MADE AT HOME
DICK & JAMES STRAWBRIDGE

BREADS

MITCHELL BEAZLEY

CONTENTS

INTRODUCTION

Once you start baking it is hard to keep focused on anything else.
A part of you may try to continue with your daily routine -- work on
another job, or relax with a book -- but your mind will keep coming
back to your dough and the magnetic urge to check on its progress.
The history of baking has risen alongside civilization itself and it is
a human activity that is almost instinctive. In the past, baking was
often a community event and large bread ovens would be fired up and
stocked with an entire community's bread. This coming together still
goes on in many countries around the world and to some extent we
still witness it in our home. When a loaf comes out of the oven at our
house people gather for a warm slice with some cold butter.

The skills required to bake a wide range of different breads are
challenging, but grounded in a simple set of ratios and techniques
which have been developed over hundreds of years. Our approach to
baking is to fit it into our lifestyle, creatively developing flavours and
meals where bread is a key part, not just served in a basket on the
side. We bake it because it is fun, exciting, addictive and healthy.
There are times when a commercial loaf from the local shop would
be easier, but it is never as satisfying to eat.

FAST LIFE, SLOW FOOD

While there are plenty of recipes in this book for breads that can
be baked in no time at all, generally speaking baking bread is
not a quick process. The secret is choosing the right time to bake.
A standard loaf requires planning, patience and waiting while

the natural process works its magic. Our advice is to enjoy the pace of bread; the time kneading dough or waiting for it to rise is precious and nowadays there are very few activities that give us the opportunity to slow down.

The earlier you start making your bread in the morning, the more likely it can fit into a daily routine. If you go out to work early every day, then try making slow-fermented breads like sourdough. These natural breads benefit from extra time to mature and grow. Alternatively, bake late at night and the next day you will enjoy the best breakfast imaginable. If you are really busy but still have caught the baking bug, bake larger batches of bread at the weekend and freeze them for convenience.

BE AN ARTISAN

There is a huge revival in baking that must make many of our grandparents smile. We like this domestic pride and renaissance in bread. In fact, it's another classic example of people taking more responsibility for their own food. The excellent thing about the artisan way of baking is that it celebrates individuality instead of the uniform bread of commercial factories. This also happens to be a great excuse for any small mistakes that you make while learning the art of baking. We love the odd loaf that comes out of the oven looking different, as it is part of the learning process and a talking point. Experimentation with textures and taste combinations puts the art into artisan. To truly master bread, practice bakes perfect.

BREAD & FAMILY LIFE

We have absorbed baking influences from all corners of our family and from all over the world. Bread is universal and there are so many cultural traditions to play with. One batch of dough can easily be shaped into a variety of different rolls, loaves or braids. Sitting around the table and preparing to start your day with a slice of toast or a muffin with a free-range egg on top is a taste of the good life that is comforting and familiar.

We have kneaded baking into our family life so that the hearth is once again the focal point of our home. If you want to feed a hungry teenager quality bread to fuel them, or bake tasty bread sticks to wean your child, indulge your partner with a romantic dinner or impress guests with an irresistible aroma, then bread baked at home is the key. Keep alive your family traditions by asking your relatives about their bread memories and pass them on to your children. After all, playing with dough is messy, fun and creative -- perfect for an early education in food.

HEALTH & HAPPINESS

The joy of bread is different for different people: it may be smelling the yeasty aroma of a fresh loaf in the oven, tearing a still-steaming rustic roll and sharing it with a friend, or the satisfied grin of a baker admiring a batch of golden rolls cooling on a rack covered with a shiny crust of success. Happiness for us is about eating delicious food. Good food is our motivation for all the work we do digging in the garden or sourcing ingredients to cook with. The good news is that with home baking, good food comes cheap. Some bits of equipment require a little investment but flour and yeast are still affordable and baking is not an expensive hobby.

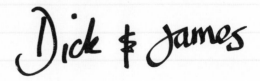

PREPARING TO

BAKE

Deciding that you like the idea of baking and knowing where to start are two different things. The world of bread is massive and there's a whole vocabulary to learn, which differs from country to country and even from baker to baker. Our advice is not to get hung up on the specifics, but to practise the basics and try to grasp the theory. Once you understand a bit of the technical side, there is a huge range of bread that you can try. Start at the beginning of this book rather than diving in at the deep end. After following a few recipes for basic loaves, you will feel confident enough to move on to your favourites.

HANDMADE AT HOME

Bread is a combination of simple ingredients that are mixed together, baked and transformed into food. We believe that making bread at home is about keeping it uncomplicated. We prefer to work our dough by hand and avoid bread machines and food processors. They do have a role if you are in a serious rush but, for us, part of the fun in baking is taking time to just bake.

The other benefit of working by hand is that you know exactly when your dough is ready to move on to the next step and when to work it for longer. Bread machines are an excellent tease into the world of baking and some people swear by them, but the uniform loaf that will come out after baking doesn't inspire us in the same way. Our advice is to get your hands dirty and work the dough.

NATURAL INGREDIENTS

We prefer natural ingredients to artificial alternatives. Sadly, though, unless you are buying from a decent artisan baker it is hard to avoid artificial additives, raising agents and preservatives in commercial bread. Most mass-produced bread contains a list of nasty chemicals that you wouldn't allow into your baking cupboard. We use a selection of stone-ground flours to make our bread, which are produced using a waterwheel. If you can find a supplier of natural flour (you may need to search online), you'll be pleasantly surprised by the great taste.

FLATBREADS

Historically, these unleavened breads are the oldest and most global. People make bread with just flour and water all around the world. Different types of flour provide very different colours and textures and the methods for shaping, rolling and baking flatbreads are diverse. Flatbreads are great to serve with rich curries, roll up and wrap around food as an alternative sandwich, dip in sauces or stuff with tasty treats. Many bakers will insist that the only way to shape flatbread is to use your hands. We have tried this traditional approach but prefer to use a rolling pin. Baking options are great fun, and these breads are suitable for outdoor grilling and barbecues.

BREADS MADE FROM STARTERS

Before adopting specialist baking yeasts to make bread, people developed cultures of natural yeasts and used flour and water to develop a 'starter'. There are huge benefits to using starters in baking. Many people who are intolerant of yeast and wheat flour can enjoy a loaf of sourdough bread without as many issues due to the slow growth and structure of the dough. The other attractive element is that once you mix together a batch of starter, you don't need to go out and buy yeast.

Starters involve looking after a living organism – the yeasts that develop need regular care so this type of bread isn't for everyone. We find that a weekly refreshing of our starter is a quick and easy chore to add into our routine. Plus, the taste and chewy texture of bread made with starters is very special and worth the extra effort. Starters can offer an array of random bubbles in a farmhouse loaf or, if you have an intolerance of wheat flour, they are excellent mixed with rye flour to create dark, dense loaves.

BREADS MADE WITH YEAST

Yeast is the ingredient that aerates dough with amazing bubbles, adds unique flavour and allows it to rise into a large and impressive loaf. Yeast likes very exact conditions to thrive but luckily these are very similar to the environment that we enjoy living in – a warm room is ideal. We have a real soft spot for yeast breads as they have huge flexibility and can be tailored to suit a range of dishes. You can use yeast to make flavoured breads, rolls and baguettes, oily breads like pizza or focaccia, and even sweet breads infused with spices and fruit. To succeed when baking with yeast, try to care for it and nurture it through the different stages of the baking process.

QUICK BREADS

Yeast needs time to grow and develop, and that can sometimes be hard to fit into a working day. Quick breads are our answer for busy times when we still want to bake. Quick breads are among our favourite bread recipes: they are simple and great for building confidence.

EQUIPPING YOURSELF

Unlike many other forms of cookery, baking is not a friend to improvisation. If you get too adventurous and change the quantities then you can end up with a loaf that looks or tastes terrible. This is why a set of good scales is vital. The tools and equipment required are all concerned with accuracy and a fairly clinical approach. Baking is simple and there's a reason why many recipes haven't changed for hundreds of years. Attention to detail and working by hand are our preferred methods.

1

BAKING
BASICS

INTRODUCTION TO
BAKING BASICS

To make delicious bread, you need to start with quality ingredients. The formula for a tasty loaf involves good flour, yeast, salt and water. The better the flour, the more aromatic your bread will be and the better it will rise and bake. We use organic flour wherever possible to avoid the use of chemicals, and if there's a choice we use spring water instead of tap water. However, wherever you get your ingredients, you are still going to bake healthier, cheaper bread than anything you can buy. How good it tastes is down to your skill and experience, but we'll help along the way by offering plenty of tips and advice.

FLOUR

The main ingredient in bread is flour. We choose locally milled organic flour but have no problems occasionally using conventional bleached flour for a classic white loaf.

WHEAT FLOUR

There are many different types of flour. The most common is wheat flour. Wheat grains contain loads of flavour and are packed with vitamins, protein, starches and sugars, plus valuable minerals and oils. These all work together and feed off each other during the fermentation process to develop a strong gluten structure. This means that wheat flour is perfect for using in yeast breads.

- Strong flour is superb for baking bread. It has more proteins and therefore gives you a higher percentage of gluten in the dough. Strong flour can come in wholemeal, white or brown.
- Malted flour contains grains that have started to germinate, which produces plenty of extra sugar. Then they are dried and roasted to give them that distinctive brown colour.
- 00 flour is a fine Italian flour made from durum wheat. It is perfect for making pasta but can also be used in focaccia or ciabatta.

OTHER GRAINS

Bread doesn't have to contain just wheat flour; other grains can be used too.

- Spelt is similar to wheat and makes excellent bread. It contains slightly less gluten and is thought to be easier to digest, making it popular with people who are intolerant of wheat. Spelt flour is usually brown but you can buy white spelt flour in some health food shops and online.
- Rye flour doesn't have as much gluten in it so it is very popular with those intolerant of wheat. Rye bread is normally dense and doesn't rise as much. It is perfect for making a sourdough bread because the naturally occurring yeasts will add acidity to a fairly bland flour and the resulting loaf will last for a long time.
- Cornflour is excellent for flatbreads. We don't bake with it very often but do enjoy dusting loaves with it for a richly coloured crust.

you can bake with a wide variety of flours and grains

WATER

Normal mains water is fine for most baking, although if you are trying to develop your own starter then filter the water to avoid any chlorine or chemicals that may interfere with the beneficial bacteria in your culture. The temperature is important and, as a rule, tepid water is best.

YEAST

Dried yeast keeps for several months and is reliable and fairly consistent unless near the end of its shelf-life. The powder quickly dissolves in tepid water and takes less time to activate than fresh yeast. However, we prefer using fresh yeast as it has less packaging and can be crumbled into the flour. Buy yeast in small batches so that it stays fresh. Keep fresh yeast wrapped in clingfilm in the refrigerator for no longer than 2 weeks. After this it will turn from a pleasant pale mushroom colour to a dark, rancid-smelling lump of dry putty.

SALT

Salt is excellent at preserving food and it will keep your bread free from mould for longer. It also has an important role tightening the gluten structure and making your dough stronger and better at supporting the weight of itself. The salt allows precious bubbles to be held in the dough and also keeps the bread soft for longer. Too much salt inhibits the growth of yeast, so never use more than is specified in a recipe. We often use coarse sea salt because it is always in our kitchen but fine salt will spread better through the dough.

TOOLS & EQUIPMENT

You will probably already have most of the equipment you need to make a start: rolling pin, measuring jug, whisk, wooden spoon, pastry brush, wire cooling rack and some baking sheets. The other things you may need are listed below; all are relatively inexpensive but you may need to go online or to a specialist shop to get hold of some of them.

SCALES

Scales are essential for making bread. We prefer modern digital scales which you can reset to zero before adding the next ingredient to the mixing bowl. The more accurate the better – opt for scales which are sensitive to at least 5g, 2g if possible.

CLOTHS

Tea towels are useful in many aspects of baking and fine mesh ones are better than fluffy cotton types. If you have linen tea towels, reserve these for baking and flour them well. A generous covering of flour means that you can line proving baskets or cover dough as it rises without it sticking. Tea towels are also excellent for dividing rolls so they don't stick to each other when they are proving. Make a pleat in the towel so that there is a barrier between dough balls. A damp tea towel can also be laid over a mixing bowl or proving basket to stop the dough drying out as it rises. Re-wet it at intervals so that the mesh doesn't allow too much air to pass through. An alternative for covering dough is clingfilm or reused plastic bags.

DOUGH SCRAPERS

The one tool that we wouldn't be without is a plastic dough scraper. The spatula shape is excellent for cleaning out a mixing bowl, lifting dough on to a surface, scraping up any sticky parts and dividing into rough shapes. Normally they are made from flexible plastic and have one curved edge and a straighter side. It won't take much baking before you fall in love with your dough scraper, but you could happily manage without one. Another type of scraper, often known as a Scottish scraper, is a stainless-steel rectangle with a handle on one of the long sides. It is used for dividing dough into rolls or smaller loaves.

WATER MISTER

Water is important at many stages of baking and a water mister is invaluable. Buy a refillable mister from a garden centre, keep it near the oven and use it to spray your dough before and after it goes into the oven. The fine mist will add instant humidity to your oven and evenly cover the surface of the dough to help form a good crust.

MIXING BOWLS

Mixing bowls are essential for making bread. We prefer ceramic bowls, but any mixing bowl is suitable. Glass, wood and earthenware bowls are the best insulators and will keep your dough nice and cosy. Keep metal bowls away from direct heat, such as a radiator or oven, when you are leaving the dough to rise. The heat conducted can give an uneven temperature in the dough and cause problems later on.

PROVING BASKETS

Breads with less gluten tend to need more support as they prove. If you want the right kit for these loaves, buy a couple of proving baskets, sometimes referred to as bannetons. These are often lined with linen cloths and can be made from wicker, wood pulp or plastic. Dust them well with flour before use and don't worry about washing them.

KNIVES, RAZORS & LAMES

Slashing the dough is a necessary step for many loaves before they go in the oven. A sharp bread knife, razor or baker's lame

is useful for making fine cuts into the surface of the dough.

LOAF TINS

If you plan to make bread in a traditional loaf shape, you will need loaf tins. The most popular sizes are 500g (1lb) and 1kg (2lb) tins; choose whichever size suits your needs. We take precautions to keep our loaf tins in good condition. To prevent rust and keep them for years, we rub a light oil over the metal surface after use and then wrap each tin in greaseproof paper. Stack them inside one another until you need to use them.

OVEN

Before you begin baking, place a thermometer in your oven while it is hot and measure the actual temperature compared to what the dial says it should be. Often oven dials are inaccurate and this can make a big difference to your baking.

Baking temperatures are described in the table below. These descriptions below are for standard ovens; if you have a fan-assisted oven, check the manufacturer's instructions to adjust the temperature accordingly.

OVEN TEMPERATURES

°C	°F	GAS MARK	DESCRIPTION
140	275	1	Cool
160	325	3	Warm
180	350	4	Moderate
200	400	6	Hot
230	450	8	Very Hot

MAKING DOUGH

If bread is a house, then the bricks and mortar are the ingredients in the dough. Mixing to the right consistency and with the right balance of components is vital. It will take practice if you are a first-time baker but it's worth it! You'll start to learn when the dough is at the right level of elasticity, how to adjust temperatures of ingredients depending on the time of year, or whether you need a drop more water in your dough. The key is patience and hard work. You can mix dough in a machine but we prefer to do it by hand. The whole process is grounding and really lets you get to know your ingredients.

PREPARING

Start by preparing your work area so that there is a degree of order. We like to have all of the ingredients within easy reach and scales set on an even surface. If possible, choose scales that can be reset to zero after each ingredient has been weighed. This allows you to weigh everything together in one bowl and saves on washing up. The magic of science means that 1ml of water weighs 1g, so you can even weigh your liquid too if you prefer.

MAKING

For a basic bread dough, set a mixing bowl on the scales and weigh the flour into it. Sometimes a recipe will call for you to sift in the flour – this simply involves pouring it into a sieve set over the bowl and tapping it gently to pass it through. For a basic loaf you can skip this step.

To add fresh yeast to the dough, simply crumble it into the flour and use your fingertips to rub the flour and yeast together. Work the mixture for a few minutes until the yeast is a fine crumb. If using dried or fast-acting yeast, follow the packet instructions.

Add the salt to the bowl carefully so that you don't put in too much by mistake. Now pour in the water slowly, unless you have already added it with the dried yeast. In summer, tepid water may feel cold and in winter it may feel warmer. To be safe you could use a thermometer to check the temperature – it should ideally be 28–30°C (82–86°F) – but we aren't that precious.

Other ingredients that you add to the dough mixture, such as butter, lard, olive oil or eggs, should be at room temperature. If they are too cold it will take longer for the yeast to increase and bread to rise.

MIXING

The dough can be mixed with a wooden spoon, your hands, a machine or with a dough scraper. This stage normally takes 3–4 minutes. If using a scraper, scrape down the sides of the bowl and into the middle. Move the mixture around and fold the dough over itself until you start to feel a structure being established. When you feel that the dough is soft but no longer pooling with water, you are ready to start kneading.

HOW TO MAKE DOUGH

Weigh the flour into a large bowl. Crumble in the yeast and rub in with the fingertips until the mixture resembles fine breadcrumbs. Add the salt and stir well.

Pour the water into the bowl and use a dough scraper to start incorporating it into the flour.

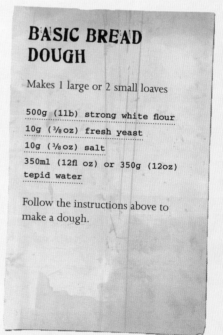

BASIC BREAD DOUGH

Makes 1 large or 2 small loaves

500g (1lb) strong white flour

10g (⅜oz) fresh yeast

10g (⅜oz) salt

350ml (12fl oz) or 350g (12oz) tepid water

Follow the instructions above to make a dough.

Work the dough for 3–4 minutes until smooth and soft. Time spent now will reduce the effort of kneading, so give it a good mix.

The air kneading technique

METHOD #2

KNEADING

Of all the stages of bread making, kneading is the part that makes you feel like you've earned a slice from the final loaf. It is a good honest activity that requires skill, practice and motivation. There are two main techniques: air kneading involves aerating the dough by pulling it up towards you and then flipping it down on itself, while traditional kneading involves pushing and pulling the dough until smooth. Choose whichever you prefer.

PREPARING

Make sure the work surface is very clean before you start. Then comes the baker's dilemma: 'To flour or not to flour?' Flouring a work surface before kneading will prevent the dough sticking but the flour you sprinkle on the work surface will become incorporated into the dough and affect the balance of ingredients. The truth is that it is a matter of personal preference and developing an eye for your dough. If the dough is too wet then a little flour on the surface will make it easier to work and you'll end up with a nice lump of dough. However, if the dough already feels perfect or a little on the dry side, work on an unfloured surface. The flour in the dough absorbs water as it is kneaded and the gluten starts to develop a strong structure. As your dough becomes more elastic, it will stick less to the surface and more to itself.

AIR KNEADING

Place the dough on a work surface and hold the side closest to you between the thumb and forefingers of each hand. With your thumbs pulling the dough from the bottom, bring your hands up and towards you in one smooth movement. When the dough has stretched as far as it will, flip your hands forwards to fold the dough over itself in a slapping motion. Eventually you will find that the dough will stretch almost up to your shoulders before lifting off the work surface. Rotate the dough and tuck in the edges as you go so it is kneaded evenly.

TRADITIONAL KNEADING

Start by vigorously stretching the dough out in front of you with the heel of your hand. Push it down into the surface so that you are really working the flour structure. It will tear and stick but continue for 2–3 minutes. Pull the dough back towards you after each motion with closed fingers and push in a slightly different direction.

Now start the more focused and therapeutic kneading. This can be done alternating hands so that one arm doesn't get too tired but you'll find that you probably prefer one arm over the other. Push the ball of dough forwards away from you with the heel of your hand and as you pull it back towards you, rotate the dough with your other hand. Then repeat and repeat; as you are moving the dough you will find your own rhythm.

Continue kneading for 8–10 minutes until the dough becomes smooth, elastic and shiny. You can over-knead dough so don't get carried away. Once it feels right, do the window test to see if it's ready.

WINDOW TEST

The window test is a simple technique to see if the dough has been kneaded enough. It works with white bread dough, but not rye or wholemeal. Stretch the dough between your fingers: if you can stretch it into a thin film that almost lets light through, then it is ready for shaping. If not, knead the dough some more.

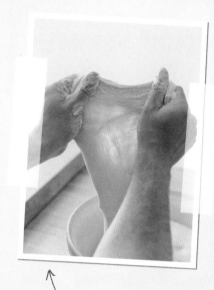

stop kneading when you can see the light

HOW TO KNEAD - THE TRADITIONAL METHOD

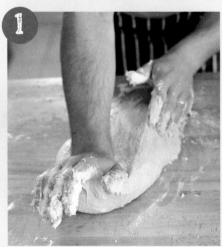

First knead vigorously for 2–3 minutes, stretching the dough with the heel of your hand until it stops tearing and sticking.

Now start the real work: knead the dough with one hand while rotating it with the other in a rhythmical movement for 8–10 minutes.

RISING & KNOCKING BACK

Good things come to those who bake. Waiting for your bread to mysteriously increase in size demands patience. We use the time to get on with other things and it means that baking can fit well into a busy lifestyle. There are ways of speeding up the process, but the longer you leave it the more the flavour will develop and the more digestible the bread will become.

RISING

This is essential as it allows the yeast in the dough to ferment. As the yeast ferments, the gluten develops structure and ripens to make the dough extra stretchy. This stretchy dough is the ideal consistency for retaining all of the carbon dioxide gas produced by the yeast, and this gas makes the bubbles in the dough, which make the bread light.

Allowing the dough time to rise also develops more flavour. Bread tastes of bread due to the by-products of fermentation. The complex acids and enzymes all add a unique taste that is lacking in most commercially made bread. The organic acids that add flavour and help the dough develop structure as it rises can take a long time to develop so patience is the key here.

If you don't have the time for a long, slow rise, using a starter can be an excellent way to add flavour quickly. The slowly ripened starter already contains this flavour and will give the dough a head start as it rises. See page 60 for more details on making a starter to add to your dough.

DOUBLE THE DOUGH

Flour a mixing bowl before placing the dough inside to rise. If you are making an olive oil bread, you can oil the bowl instead. You then need to cover the dough to prevent it drying out. You can sprinkle it lightly with flour, or use clingfilm or a tea towel over the top of the bowl. A large bin bag or plastic bag can also be used to enclose the bowl, especially if you're baking a big batch. When the dough is covered, leave in a warm place to rise. The ideal temperature for a basic dough to rise is 27°C (80°F) but it isn't crucial. Ideally, try to keep the dough warm but avoid direct

Clingfilm allows you to watch the dough's progress

KNOCKING BACK

Knocking back improves the structure of the dough and reactivates the yeast. Yeast will cease to ferment further once there is too much carbon dioxide in the dough so you need to expel some of the gas and stretch the membranes again and allow even more bubbles to form, giving your dough plenty of open texture.

There are a few different methods for knocking back; try them out and see which you prefer.

- Briefly knead the dough for 15–30 seconds. This is a great way to remove excess carbon dioxide, develop further dough strength and stretch the gluten strands. This method also mixes the dough to make the temperature even throughout, resulting in an even rise when proving.
- Generally, a wetter dough should be folded rather than kneaded. Flour the surface but avoid incorporating too much raw flour into the dough as this can lead to grey streaks when you shape it. To fold, start by mentally dividing the dough into thirds from front to back. Stretch the far third of the dough away from you a little and then bring it back and fold it over the middle third. Avoid stretching the dough too far and tearing it. Now fold the nearest third over the top of the other two. Repeat with the two sides, and pat down each time to de-gas the dough.
- Another technique, particularly suited to focaccia, is to use the fingertips to gently dimple the dough down to expel the air, pushing rather than stretching.
- Punching the air out of risen dough is another popular approach and effective for expelling gas. It doesn't, however, mix the dough or evenly distribute the temperature.

heat above a radiator or wood-burner as this can excite the dough and make it difficult to handle. Additionally, don't panic if your kitchen is not warm. As long as it isn't very cold the worst that can happen is that your dough will take a couple of hours longer to rise. However, you don't want the dough to be sitting near a draught as this can leave dough with a dry skin, which will affect the quality of bread.

Many bakers use a professional piece of kit called a proofer in which to allow their dough to rise, but a cheaper option is an electric plant propagator. Place the dough on a trivet to avoid contact with the heat underneath and spray inside the base with a water mister for added humidity. Then cover with the lid and allow the low-level heat to work its magic. If the dough is kept warm, it will take 1–2 hours to rise. It is ready when it has doubled in size. If you gently press down on the dough with a finger, it should make an indentation. If this takes a few seconds to spring back, then the dough is ready.

SHAPING

The distinctive shape of a loaf has the power to excite your tastebuds. If you are faced with the choice between a loaf tin classic, a tapered baton or a set of unique rolls, you will be drawn not by the flavour and dough type but by their appearance. Set forms suit certain breads, but we enjoy mixing up the shapes of our loaves. Variety is the spice of life.

PREPARING THE WORK SURFACE

Lightly flour the surface so that the dough doesn't stick but avoid incorporating extra flour into the folds of the dough. Floured hands are perfect for shaping, but you may need to use a dough scraper when working with wetter doughs like ciabatta.

FIRM BUT FAIR

To avoid expelling all of the air from your dough, treat it carefully but firmly. That said, you do often need to start by flattening the dough into a rectangle or oval shape. Do this with your fingertips or by patting it down with the heel of your hand.

HOW TO SHAPE A TIN LOAF

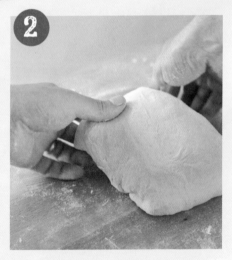

Flatten the dough into an oval the width of the tin, then roll up.

Tuck the ends of the dough underneath and roll to and fro until smooth. Carefully lower, seam side down, into a greased loaf tin.

HOW TO SHAPE A ROUND LOAF

This is a classic shape which, once baked, offers large slices with beautiful curved edges. Although the round shape may look easy, it is surprisingly testing to master.

A small amount of tackiness on the surface will help provide some traction for the shape to form but avoid tearing off the surface by dusting your hands regularly with flour throughout the process. Lightly dust the work surface with flour before you begin.

When you are tucking the dough in on itself, try to avoid trapping air. Instead of simply folding the dough over, fold, press and knead it together into a round. This avoids a large air pocket that can expand when baked later.

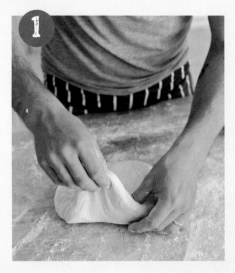

Form the dough into a round, place good side down and pat out the air. Fold the dough over on itself from the edges to the centre and tuck in. Turn over so that the seam side is down.

Place your hands around the dough so that your little fingers and wrists are in contact with the work surface. Then cup around the dough and overlap your thumbs on top.

Rotate your hands in smooth circles, keeping them parallel, and turning the dough with them. Slowly bring your little fingers in until you have a tight, seamless ball.

HOW TO SHAPE A BATON

An oval is a useful shape to perfect. This is the way that we start to shape our dough for a loaf tin and it can easily be adapted to taper more at the ends and make a baton. The key is to keep it tight by performing more folds than you'd expect. Extra work will give you a tight loaf that bakes well. Lightly flour the work surface before you begin and gently flatten the dough into a square.

The tighter the folds, the more likely your bread will prove evenly and look like a uniform baton. The reason that we make folds across at different angles is to keep the surface tension in more than one direction. But when you slash a baton just before baking it will want to unroll - hence the distinctive diagonal cut across the top of a baguette.

Fold the far edge of the dough on to an imaginary centre line running across the dough. Fold the 2 far corners on to the same line, then rotate the dough by 180° and repeat.

HOW TO SHAPE ROLLS

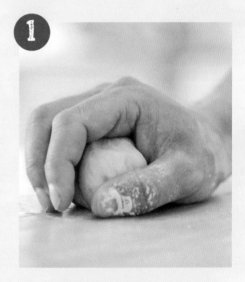

Shaping rolls is great fun, as soon as you master the technique. The process is simple but difficult to describe until you feel the magic moment when the dough fights back and firms up. Rolling 2 at a time is one of the baker's party tricks because it is a bit like patting your head and rubbing your tummy. The coordination to move your hands in different directions makes it complicated but it is a quick and efficient way to shape bread. Start by placing the dough pieces, seam side down, on a floured work surface.

Cup your flour-dusted hand over the dough. Keep your thumb and little finger in contact with the work surface and your palm on top of the dough throughout.

Now fold the top third of the dough down to cover the folds and press it down with the heel of your hand. Rotate by 180° and repeat, then turn the baton over seam side down.

Place flat hands over the centre of the dough and roll with downward pressure backwards and forwards. Gradually push your hands away from each other to elongate the dough.

Move your hand in tight circles with firm downward pressure. If the dough tears and sticks you'll need more flour. Keep going until you feel the dough tighten and take shape.

If you are shaping 2 at once, move your left hand clockwise and your right anti-clockwise. When the dough starts to withstand the pressure, the roll has been formed.

METHOD #5

PROVING

Proving is the final rising of the shaped dough before baking. You may think that with all of the stages that it takes to get your dough to this point, the hard work is over. However, proving is a skill that will govern the results of your final loaf. The good news is that with time and finger-training you can easily learn to observe the signs and perfect the art of proving.

PREPARING

The dough requires the same environment for proving as it did for the initial rising (see pages 24–5). It is essential at this stage that you avoid draughts and chills.

It is vital that you prevent the skin of the dough drying out. If it cannot stretch, the crust can tear in the oven and will not have a good texture. You can sprinkle a little flour on the dough to prevent drying or inflate a plastic bag with your moisture-laden breath

and put the tray or proving basket in it. Alternatively, use clingfilm brushed with oil to cover the dough.

THE FINGER TEST

Leave the dough for anything from 20 minutes to 4 hours, depending on the recipe and the temperature, until almost doubled in size. Test the feel of your dough at intervals while trying not to expose it to dry air for too long. Gently prod the surface with your finger and see how the dough responds. At the beginning of the prove, the indentation quickly disappears. Later you will start to feel more resistance as the gases build up in the dough. When it is ready, the dough will have changed from feeling springy to feeling more fragile. This is the time to get it in the oven.

PROVING OPTIONS

- **Loaf tin:** Proving in a loaf tin is a solid and reliable method. It is also extremely easy to gauge the volume change by looking at the level of the tin.
- **Baking sheet:** Brush the baking sheet with a little oil so the dough doesn't stick, and place the tray in an inflated bag or drape a well-floured tea towel or piece of clingfilm

brushed with oil over the top to prevent the dough drying.

- **Proving basket:** These come in many different styles: the French banneton tends to be circular and is made of coiled wicker that imprints a distinctive pattern as the bread proves, while the Germanic brotform is elongated and often oval in shape. Flour well before each use and cover the dough.

- **Tea towel:** A well-used clean tea towel or linen cloth is a great surface to prove on, especially useful for baguettes and rolls. Make pleats and folds in the cloth to stop the shapes sticking together.

- **Peel:** A baker's peel is made of wood or metal and shaped rather like a shovel. Flour the peel generously before putting the dough on it to prove, then cover the dough as above. When the dough is ready, slide it off the peel on to a hot baking stone waiting in the oven.

HOW TO PROVE DOUGH

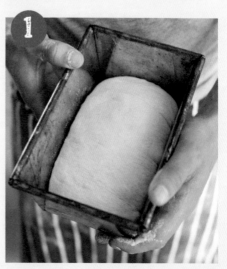

Transfer the dough to a prepared loaf tin, proving basket, peel, tea towel or baking tray. Place it seam side down unless using a basket.

Cover the loaf with a plastic bag and inflate by gently blowing air into it, ensuring that no part of the covering is in contact with the dough to prevent sticking.

Leave in a warm place until the dough has nearly doubled in size and passes the finger test. A basic white loaf will take about 45 minutes to prove in a warm place.

SCORING & COATING

When the dough has finished proving it is ready for the oven. However, there is a small window of opportunity to make the bread look and bake even better. Scoring or slashing the top of the dough quickly before it bakes is an important skill to develop. The act of cutting into the dough is the baker's way to control the final shape of the loaf. If it isn't scored the crust can bubble, tear or pop in weird places. This is also the time to add a delicious coating of seeds, nuts, cheese or a dusting of flour to add character to the final loaf.

SCORING

Dough expands in the oven as it bakes and the area with the least surface tension will be the place where the dough breaks through. By deliberately slashing the surface of the dough, you can control where this will be. When you score dough, hold the bread firmly with one hand and slice through in long, smooth cuts. Try not to push down or you will squeeze the air out.

Use a bread knife or razor for straight cuts, and a baker's lame for curved cuts. Cut to an average depth of about 1cm (½ inch). Scissors are also useful for cutting dough: in a loaf tin start at one end and make a series of cuts across the top of the dough.

DOS & DON'TS

- Do be very careful and cut safely. Although you need to work fast to get the dough in the oven, make sure you stay calm.
- Don't score round rolls unless they are very large.
- Don't score dough with a high percentage of rye flour or low-gluten dough as these breads expand very little in the oven.
- Don't cut too deep or the dough may fold back in on itself with the sheer weight and you will end up with less crust.
- Don't make very shallow cuts as they will disappear before you even get the dough in the oven.

ROUND LOAVES

For a round loaf, make straight cuts with a bread knife, slicing across the top with a small set of parallel lines. This will open the crust across the thicker parts of dough. Another

option is to make a second set of cuts at right angles so that you end up with an intricate checked pattern and very textured surface. Alternatively, use scissors to make a series of cuts from the middle of the loaf to the shoulder, radiating out in a rustic star pattern. The bread will open up like a flower and provide lots of flavoursome crust to enjoy.

LONG LOAVES

An oval loaf looks good with a single cut from end to end. It can be even more impressive if you curve the cut in at one end and out at the other to form an elongated S-shape.

BAGUETTES

Baguettes have lots of lateral tension across the surface of the dough because they have been rolled up and want to unroll when they expand. Make the most of this by opening them up with small cuts. A lengthways cut would open up too much and cause problems. Crossways cuts open less and leave you with little or no decent crust. A series of diagonal cuts is a good compromise that guarantees the best results.

A traditional practice is to score the surface of the loaf to resemble an ear of grain. Use a razor or curved lame to make a series of curved cuts from the middle of the dough to the side, alternating to left and right as you pass along the loaf. Keep the blade at an angle of 45° to the surface of the dough and aim to create a series of fairly thin flaps as deep cuts can collapse back on themselves quickly due to the weight of the dough.

COATING

There are many different options for coating the top of a loaf, from a dusting of flour to a sprinkling of seeds, herbs or cheese. A coating can be added before or after scoring, depending on the visual effect you want to achieve. If you coat a loaf before scoring, the coating will not end up in the score marks; if you add the coating after scoring, it will cover the top of the loaf evenly. The coating can also be applied through a simple cardboard stencil. Hold the stencil close to the dough and dust from above.

METHOD #7

BAKING

Baking is the time when all your hard works hits your senses. Your kitchen will be soaked in the amazing aroma of fresh bread and soon you'll get the ultimate satisfaction of slicing into your loaf and eating it. Unfortunately, domestic ovens aren't really suited to bread baking because they have very little insulation and are designed for dry cooking, not a moist environment (old-fashioned kiln ovens like Agas are an exception). Don't panic -- we have found that you can still form a decent crust on your bread, but only if you attack it with steam and try some other rather underhand baking techniques!

INTO THE OVEN

One of our favourite parts of baking bread is the final transformation in the oven. The dough will rise again and change into a richly coloured bread ready to eat with friends and family. The yeast will activate for another fermentation and the bread will rise, expanding with trapped gases and steam. Then the rising temperature will kill off the yeast and the enzymes will work overtime, converting the colour of the crust. Starch on the surface converts into a gelatinized gloss, and at last the colour deepens with caramelization. All of this magic happens while you wait for the final time.

PREHEATING

As already mentioned, the temperature on an oven's dial and the actual internal temperature can vary considerably. It is worth starting by testing the temperature and adjusting your timings or dial accordingly. Ideally, the temperature should be 220°C (425°F) when the bread goes in. If it is only reading 200°C (400°F), turn the dial up a little and test the temperature again. Alternatively, give the bread a little longer in the oven.

Place a roasting tin in the bottom of the oven, and a baking stone if you are using one, while the oven preheats. You can place a few ice cubes into the tin to moisten the oven before baking.

STEAM

All bread benefits from steam during baking and commercial bread ovens have steam-injectors built into them. Spray the dough with a fine water mister before it goes into the oven. Then, once the bread is in the oven, spray it again or tip a cup of just-boiled water into the roasting tin. Do this quickly but safely, wearing gloves and long sleeves to protect against the steam if necessary. Close the door and do not open again for 10 minutes.

The steam produced not only adds colour and shine to the surface but also helps the bread to increase in volume. Water in contact with the dough will cool the surface and allow the enzymes to remain active for longer. These enzymes break down starches into simple sugars that can contribute to a good colour. The water also keeps the dough moist for longer, which slows down the formation of the crust and allows the dough underneath to expand and create a bigger loaf.

USING A BAKING STONE & PEEL

A baking stone is a heavy slab of stone which is preheated in the oven and retains heat extremely well. The bread is baked directly on the stone. The act of sliding a loaf smoothly on to a baking stone is similar to pulling a tablecloth out from under crockery without spilling a bowl of soup. If you have used a floured peel for your dough to prove on, lay the edge of the peel in the middle of the stone at a downwards angle and then in

one movement slide your arm forward and snap it back at whipping speed. When you get this right the loaf will sit perfectly in the middle of the stone. When you get it wrong, reposition the loaf and close the oven door.

OVEN SPRING

The final fermentation of the dough occurs inside the oven as the bread bakes. The remaining yeast will quickly convert the last of its food and the bread will rise again. Bakers call this 'oven spring'. The water remaining in the dough will turn to steam and increase the volume. This is why a loaf that comes out of the oven weighs typically 10–20% less than when it went in. Also, all of the gas bubbles inside the dough will expand and increase the volume even more.

THE CRUST

On the crust there's a whole other process at work. The steam in the oven is reacting with the amino acids and sugars on the surface of the dough, colouring the dough into an appetizing golden crust. The crust sugars will caramelize and the starch will gelatinize into a glossy surface. Bread will vary in colour according to the ingredients and, as a general rule, enriched breads with added sugar will brown more quickly. If the bread comes out with a pale crust, the chances are that you left the bread to prove too long before baking.

GLAZES

If the bread does not develop a golden, crusty exterior, it may be because your oven is not retaining enough moisture. Glazes are an excellent way round this problem. We tend to eat with our eyes and a good-looking loaf does taste better. Glazes won't greatly affect the texture of the crust, but a shiny gloss can really work wonders. Try brushing the surface of the dough before it goes into the oven with a beaten egg mixed with milk for a golden finish, a beaten egg yolk for a darker glaze, or milk alone for a subtle shine. For smooth breads, you could even mix a textured wash of 1 tablespoon of light rye flour and 4 tablespoons of boiling water, and brush on like a pottery glaze.

REDUCE THE HEAT

After 10 minutes in the oven, the crust will have formed. For breads made with starters and fermented soakers, spray the loaf again with water at this stage as these breads take longer to form a crust. For the majority of breads, it is now time to turn down the temperature of the oven to 200°C (400°F).

Below are the standard baking times for different types of bread:
- Rolls   15–20 minutes
- Small loaves   25–30 minutes
- Large loaves   40–50 minutes

COLOUR & SOUND

When the bread has finished baking, check the colour and crust. Many people knock on the bread to see if it has a hollow sound. This is not an exact science. Bread can sound hollow but be undercooked. If your bread is in a loaf tin, remove it from the tin and return it to the oven for a further 5 minutes or until the bottom takes on more colour.

COOLING

Home bakers are often tempted to enjoy warm bread straight from the oven, but most bread improves as it cools. Bread that is cut when hot will be dense and so full of steam that it may taste soggy. A good loaf of bread will benefit from being left to cool and can develop extra flavour after a period of resting. A sourdough or rye bread will benefit from being left for up to 24 hours for the flavours to mingle and the crust to settle. Leave your bread on a wire rack to cool. This will take longer for larger loafs

than rolls but is essential if you want to taste your bread at its best.

This is the culmination of your baking so enjoy it. Tear or slice your bread and taste it. This is the time to consider what you could improve on, where you made mistakes or what you'd do differently next time.

HOW TO BUILD A BREAD OVEN

The taste of bread baked in a wood-fired oven is exceptional. The baked dough takes on a smoky aroma and has a distinctive texture. The beating heart of a home used to be the hearth where bread was baked and people warmed themselves around a fire. A kitchen now holds the focus for most families but if you build a bread oven you may find that your focus shifts outside and baking becomes even more than a way of preparing food but a key ingredient in your lifestyle. We use ours primarily for small loaves of bread, flatbreads, rolls and pizzas but they can be used for

a huge range of other foods, from roasted vegetables to fish pies.

The advantage of an earth oven is its incredible heat-retaining capability. You will find a pizza or small rolls cook in just a few minutes and the oven often stays warm enough to bake a few batches of bread in succession. The cost of building one is next to nothing and the process, while a bit messy, is a lot of fun.

MAKING THE BASE
Build a firm base to support the oven. Old railway sleepers, stone or brick will do the job. Keep it level and build it up to a comfortable working height for cooking. The base must have a smooth, solid top surface. Standard red bricks or old paving slabs are ideal. If using old bricks, remove any old mortar and tamp them into a deep layer of sand, butting the edges up close together until they sit flush with one another.

MARKING THE CIRCUMFERENCE

Mark the outer circumference of the oven on your base using a marker pen. Make it as large as possible, about 60cm (24 inches) in diameter. Draw another circle about 7.5–10cm (3–4 inches) inside the first to show the thickness of the walls. Make a note of the diameter of the inner circle – you'll need it later to work out the size of the oven door.

MIXING THE CLAY

Clay can often be dug from the ground, but if you don't have any near you, buy some from a building merchant. You will need about 25kg (55lb). Sift the clay to remove pebbles and debris if necessary. Lay a big tarpaulin on the ground and place the clay on it. Take off your shoes and socks and tread it together. Add a small amount of sharp sand (about a bucketful) and some water if the clay is very dry. This takes some time and effort. Test the clay to see if it is ready to work with. Make a clay sausage and hold it with half in your palm and the other half dangling over your hand. If the clay bends but does not break, it's ready to use.

MAKING THE OVEN FLOOR

Make a 1cm (½ inch) thick layer of clay to cover the internal circle of the base. Spread the clay with a trowel, then smooth it with your hands to make a smooth base. Cover the circle with a layer of moist newspaper to stop any sand sticking to it.

SHAPING THE OVEN

Now use moist sand to make a dome on top of the wet newspaper covering the clay base. This will be the shape of the oven and will support the clay dome as it dries and be removed later. The sand dome should be 7.5–10cm (3–4 inches) taller than the radius (half the diameter) of the oven. When complete, measure the height of the sand dome, which will be the interior height of your oven, and write the number down.

COVERING THE WALLS WITH CLAY

Cover the sand dome with wet newspaper to stop the clay sticking to it. Starting at the base, cover the wet newspaper covering the sand dome with a layer of clay 7.5–10cm (3–4 inches) thick, using your pen mark as a guide. Shape the clay into small briquettes, then flatten and squash them into place, using the width of your hand as a rough guide to thickness as you work up the dome. Try to push the clay against itself, not against the sand. Cover the entire dome with clay, making sure it is still the same thickness at the top as the bottom. Wet your hands and smooth the surface of the finished dome.

CUTTING THE DOORWAY

To work out the most efficient height for the oven door, take the height of the sand dome you measured earlier (the internal height of the oven) and multiply it by 0.63. If the sand dome is 38cm (15 inches) tall, the door should be just under 24cm (9½ inches) in height. The width of the door should be about 25cm (10 inches), half the oven's internal diameter (which you noted earlier) and big enough for a small pizza to slide in and out. Use a sharp knife to cut out the door in two stages, cutting out first one half, then the other. Leave to dry for a few days or a week.

SCOOPING OUT THE SAND

Once the walls of the oven resist denting if you poke them, scoop out the sand from the oven. Repair any cracks that appear in the clay by wetting the surface and then gently scoring it with a cross-hatch pattern. Apply more

BUILDING YOUR OWN BREAD OVEN

dome-shaped earth oven

wooden door soaked in water

paving stones

timber frame

internal clay surface

wood store for easy access

clay to these cracked areas and repeat again if cracks appear after firing.

MAKING THE OVEN DOOR

Finish the oven by cutting out a paper template for the oven door. Use this to cut out a wooden door. Any kind of hardwood will do for the door; avoid composites like MDF, and resinous softwoods like pine. The door doesn't need to be a perfect fit, but a handle will help you get it out when your bread is ready. Remember to soak the door in water before putting it in place each time you cook. This will help make steam in the oven as well as stopping the door from charring.

BUILDING A WEATHERPROOF COVER

Finally, build a small removable roof or cover to protect the oven from the rain when you aren't using it. This needs to be easy to lift on and off so you aren't put off using the bread oven.

COOKING WITH AN EARTH OVEN

Light a small fire in the centre of the oven using paper (not fire lighters), bits of kindling and small seasoned logs, and leave the door open. This will heat the oven over a few hours. You'll know it's ready to cook when the soot disappears from the inside of the oven walls. Remove the coals using a small shovel or a poker and start baking. As soon as you have put your dough in to bake, put the door in to keep the oven warm. A specially sized peel makes life easy and avoids burning bread.

Practice makes perfect: each earth oven will have its own unique cooking temperature depending on the firewood you use and how thick your walls are. .

STORING

wrap bread to keep it fresh

Bread made at home has a shorter shelf-life than commercial loaves laden with artificial additives and preservatives. Fresh bread is delicious, but there is a time when bread goes stale and needs to be toasted, turned into breadcrumbs or cooked to save throwing it away. We have found that there are great methods for revitalizing old bread, preserving it as a useful ingredient and cooking delicious meals with leftovers. The key thing is to not bake too much in the first place and to store it in a suitable environment.

STORING BREAD

The best way to store bread is to first allow it to cool completely, then store it in a dark, dry environment. Avoid low temperatures (never store bread in a refrigerator); 16°C (61°F) or

above is ideal. It is also worth wrapping your bread in greaseproof paper or placing it in a plastic bag to stop it from completely drying out. A moist rye bread will last much longer than a white loaf, but it will become chewier and denser with age. Bread with more fat in it will also seem fresher for longer because the gases are retained in the crumb for longer, making it appear lighter.

REVITALIZING A TIRED LOAF

The easiest way to get a tasty snack from an ageing loaf of bread is to toast it, but there are other ways to extend the life of your loaf. The best way to revitalize a floundering loaf on the edge of staleness is to reheat it in the oven.

If you want to firm up the crust, then try a quick blast of 2–3 minutes at 200°C (400°F), Gas Mark 6. This heats the crust layer but won't permeate into the crumb inside. If you feel that your bread has lost the softness you like in the middle, lower the temperature to

160°C (325°F), Gas Mark 3, and bake for 10–12 minutes. If your bread is solid and your freezer is already full of breadcrumbs, try spraying the bread with water and wrapping it in tin foil. Then bake for 15 minutes at 160°C (325°F), Gas Mark 3, removing the foil for a crunchier crust for the last few minutes.

FREEZING

The best way to keep bread close to fresh is to freeze it. However, the process does add about a day to the staling process, so make sure you freeze it early. It's also worth slicing it before freezing as the fabric of bread does sometimes struggle to hold together when you defrost. This will also allow you to reach into the freezer and pull out a few slices without waiting for a whole loaf to defrost.

BREADCRUMBS

Breadcrumbs are a great way to use up stale bread and are particularly good frozen and sealed in freezer bags. To make your own breadcrumbs, simply put your bread into a food processor and blitz until fine, then pour the breadcrumbs into a freezer bag, gently squeeze out the air, seal the bag and place in the freezer.

Breadcrumbs will keep in the freezer for 3–4 months. You can add seasoning or dried herbs to the breadcrumbs before you freeze them. Defrost the breadcrumbs before cooking or use them straight from the freezer. Use breadcrumbs to thicken soups, fry with herbs and garlic for crunchy toppings, make into a classic bread sauce with infused milk, coat your own fish fingers, or add to a stuffing.

GREMOLATA CROUTONS

Serves 4

4 slices of stale bread, cubed
1 tablespoon olive oil
salt and freshly ground black pepper
2–3 sprigs of fresh parsley, chopped
zest of 1 lemon
2 garlic cloves, finely chopped

Place the bread in a bowl with the olive oil, season to taste and toss until evenly mixed. Place on a baking sheet and cook in a preheated oven at 200°C (400°F), Gas Mark 6, for about 10 minutes until crisp. Allow to cool, then toss with the remaining ingredients. Serve with salads or in soup.

Leftovers become the perfect garnish

2

FLATBREADS

INTRODUCTION TO

FLATBREADS

Flatbreads are perhaps the simplest of breads to bake. This is because they are normally made from just flour, water and salt. Some flatbreads may include a small amount of yeast, like pittas, but on the whole these breads are unleavened and will stay flat even when baked. We have enjoyed making our own flatbreads for years and find they offer great opportunities for flavouring the dough, stuffing them with spices or rolling them up to use as wraps. Flatbreads are delicious baked, griddled and even fried.

SHAPING

Flatbreads have been made in many places around the world for thousands of years. Many indigenous people and stringent food traditionalists use the established technique of shaping flatbreads by hand, pressing the ball of dough down with the heel of the hand and shaping it between the palms or the back of the hand. This can be great fun and, with practice, quick and easy.

We tend to opt for a more pragmatic approach and use a boring old rolling pin to shape our flatbreads. We believe that a rolling pin gives a slightly more even surface and requires less hand-to-eye coordination. The exception is if we are cooking the flatbreads outdoors somewhere and we can't find a flat surface for rolling. Whichever approach you prefer, find a technique that suits you and produces flatbreads that bake evenly.

UNIFORMITY

One rustic flatbread may look completely different from another beneath it in a pile. However, if you'd like to create more uniform breads, here's a few tips. Firstly, use scales to weigh each ball of dough rather than dividing

the dough into portions by eye. A ball of dough can vary in size depending on the way you shape it, so weight is the best gauge. Secondly, form your dough into spherical balls before flattening them. This will give you a good starting point and make it easy to roll them out in a similar fashion. Thirdly, when you are rolling out, rotate the disc of dough as you roll rather than moving the angle of rolling. This enables you to appreciate how circular or oval your dough is, and means that you can work easily in a more confined area.

THICKNESS

When making very thin flatbreads, like tortillas, there is a very useful test for assessing if the dough has been rolled enough. Bring one edge of the dough over the side of the work surface, then bend down and blow at the loose edge. If it flutters like a handkerchief then it's thin enough.

USING A GRIDDLE

Cooking on a griddle or skillet is one of the perks that comes with baking flatbreads. A griddle is a cast iron pan that can be heated up to a very high temperature and bakes bread

shape your breads by hand for the rustic look

The hot-griddle test in action

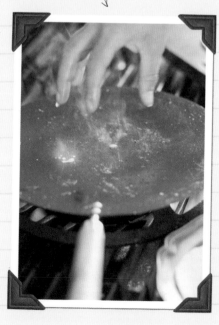

in seconds. There are ridged varieties, which can add a lovely stripe of chargrilled colour to your breads, but we prefer using a smooth-based griddle pan as it's much easier to clean and season.

One of the main benefits to using a griddle is that it requires little or no fat for baking. The heat retention of the metal also means it is excellent for baking a large number of flatbreads in one session. Preheat the griddle over a medium heat before you start cooking.

SEASONING A GRIDDLE

For a new griddle, rub a thin layer of light vegetable oil on to the cooking surface and bake in the oven for 2–3 hours on a low heat. Allow to cool to room temperature, then repeat this 2–3 times.

You also need to season your griddle each time you use it to prevent the bread from sticking to it and reduce the risk of rust. After each use, wash the griddle and place over a high heat to dry. When the water has evaporated, use kitchen paper to rub a thin layer of oil into the hot surface. Store somewhere airy, definitely not in a damp cupboard.

THE WATER TEST FOR TEMPERATURE

To see if the griddle is hot enough to start cooking, drop a few water droplets on to the surface. They should instantly sizzle and move around like raindrops on a window. If there isn't any sizzle, the griddle is not hot enough. If the water drops evaporate on impact and disappear, it is too hot, so turn down the heat, wait and retest. Never put large volumes of cold liquid into a griddle as it will crack or warp and always be careful to use oven gloves or a tea towel when picking it up.

COOKING WITH OVENS, BARBECUES & WOOD FIRES

Flatbreads are perfect for baking in an earth oven (see pages 37–9), on a barbecue or on the floor of a traditional bread oven. There is nothing quite like the taste of bread that has been infused with woody flavour or scarred with a crisscross pattern straight from the grill.

Most flatbread recipes can easily be adapted to outdoor cooking and using wood as a fuel. But remember that flatbreads will burn even quicker than a normal loaf and you may only need a few seconds on each side in a very hot oven. For really tasty results, brush the flatbreads with oil or melted butter before cooking on a barbecue or over an open fire.

If you are baking in a traditional oven, consider investing in a baking stone to really add heat to the bottom of the bread. A sprinkle of cornflour will offer that authentic look.

STAYING SOFT

After the time spent preparing and shaping the dough, the last thing you want is for your bread to turn hard and inedible just after baking. Flatbreads have a large surface area so as they cool the steam escapes very quickly and leaves the bread dry or even brittle. To avoid this and keep flatbreads more pliable, we wrap them in a tea towel as soon as they are cooked.

If you are making them in advance, allow the flatbreads to cool in the folds of a tea towel. To reheat them when you are ready to eat, either wrap in foil or mist with water and place in a hot oven for a few minutes. Alternatively, fry them in a little oil.

The baking process of a pitta bread creates an air pocket in the centre of the dough. The balloon that swells up in the oven will deflate upon cooling but the useful cavity remains. This pocket just so happens to be the perfect size for filling with chicken kebabs, salad or griddled vegetables. Our serving suggestion is a simple hummus into which to dip the fresh bread.

SERVES 4

FOR THE PITTAS

500g (1lb) strong white flour

30g (1¼oz) fresh yeast

1 teaspoon salt

50g (2oz) caster sugar

300ml (½ pint) tepid water

oil, for greasing

FOR THE HUMMUS

200g (7oz) canned chickpeas, rinsed and drained

2 tablespoons lemon juice

2 garlic cloves, crushed

100ml (3½fl oz) tahini

a pinch of salt

1 tablespoon olive oil

1 teaspoon paprika

PITTA BREAD WITH HUMMUS

To make the dough for the pittas, place the flour in a mixing bowl and crumble in the yeast. Rub the yeast into the flour with the fingertips until the mixture resembles fine breadcrumbs. Stir in the salt and sugar, then pour in the water and mix to a dough.

Knead the dough for 5–10 minutes until smooth and elastic, then return to the bowl, cover and leave to rise for 1 hour.

Preheat the oven to 230°C (450°F), Gas Mark 8, and lightly grease 2 baking sheets. Divide the dough into 100g (3½oz) lumps and roll them out into ovals about 1cm (½ inch) thick. Place 2 pittas on each prepared baking sheet and cook in the oven for 10 minutes. Wrap the cooked pittas in a tea towel and allow the oven to come up to temperature again before cooking the second batch of pittas in the same way.

If you want to freeze the pittas, remove them from the oven 2–3 minutes before they are cooked and allow to cool, then seal in an airtight bag before freezing. Defrost the pittas and return to the oven for 3–4 minutes to finish cooking.

To make the hummus, place the chickpeas, lemon juice, garlic, tahini and salt in a food processor and blend until smooth. Taste and add more lemon juice or salt if necessary. Transfer the hummus to a serving bowl, drizzle with the olive oil and sprinkle with the paprika. Serve the hummus with the warm pittas.

If you like eating curry, you've got to try making your own naan bread. We find that by adjusting the toppings, you can easily suit everyone's taste - from plain naan to garlic, peshwari or roghani. The ingredients listed for each topping are enough for 4 naans.

MAKES 4

300g (10oz) strong white flour
10g (³⁄₈oz) fresh yeast
5g (¼oz) salt
30g (1¼oz) butter or ghee, melted, plus extra for greasing and brushing
175ml (6fl oz) natural yoghurt
30ml (1¼fl oz) water

FOR GARLIC NAAN
4 garlic cloves, finely chopped
25g (1oz) butter, melted

FOR PESHWARI NAAN
25g (1oz) desiccated coconut
40g (1½oz) raisins
25g (1oz) flaked almonds
1 tablespoon caster sugar
1 teaspoon rosewater (optional)

FOR ROGHANI NAAN
3 tablespoons sesame seeds

NAAN BREAD

To make the dough, place the flour in a mixing bowl and crumble in the yeast. Rub the yeast into the flour with the fingertips until the mixture resembles fine breadcrumbs. Stir in the salt, then pour in the melted butter, yoghurt and water and mix to a dough.

Knead the dough for 5–10 minutes until smooth and elastic, then return to the greased bowl, cover and leave to rise for 1–2 hours.

Knock back the dough and divide into 4 balls. Allow to rest, covered, for 5–10 minutes. Preheat the oven to 230°C (450°F), Gas Mark 8, and place a baking stone in the oven to heat up.

Roll out the balls of dough to ovals about 5mm (¼ inch) thick and 20cm (8 inches) long. Brush with extra melted butter or ghee and sprinkle with the toppings, if using. Transfer to the baking stone in batches and cook for 5–6 minutes until puffy and golden, allowing the oven to come up to temperature again before cooking another batch.

If you want to freeze the naan breads, remove them from the oven 2–3 minutes before they are cooked and allow to cool, then seal in an airtight bag before freezing. Defrost the naans, mist with water and return to the oven for 3–4 minutes to finish cooking

Bread sticks are easy to make and provide a great excuse to create a range of different shapes with their own unique flavours. Why settle for a boring stick-shaped snack when you can play around to make an array of quirky styles?

MAKES 10

250g (8oz) strong white flour

5g (¼oz) fresh yeast

5g (¼oz) salt

175ml (6fl oz) tepid water

6-12 sun-dried tomatoes, finely chopped

50g (2oz) sesame seeds

1 tablespoon smoked paprika

olive oil, for greasing and brushing

BREAD STICKS

To make the dough, place the flour in a mixing bowl and crumble in the yeast. Rub the yeast into the flour with the fingertips until the mixture resembles fine breadcrumbs. Stir in the salt, then pour in the water and mix to a dough.

Knead the dough for 5–10 minutes until smooth and elastic, then return to the bowl, cover and leave to rise for 1 hour.

Roll out the dough to a 30 x 15cm (12 x 6 inch) rectangle, about 1 cm (½ inch) thick. Sprinkle the tomatoes, one-third of the sesame seeds and the paprika over two-thirds of the dough, then fold the bare third over the middle third. Fold the final third over the top and roll out again to the original size.

Sprinkle with half the remaining sesame seeds and cut the dough into 10 long strips. Sprinkle the remaining sesame seeds on a board and twist the dough strips into spirals on the board. To do this, pinch the ends flat and twist the ends in opposite directions until you have a tight and even spiral.

Preheat the oven to 200°C (400°F), Gas Mark 6, and lightly grease a baking sheet. Arrange the dough sticks on the prepared baking sheet, cover and leave to prove for 20 minutes. Spray the dough sticks with a water mister and cook in the oven for 10 minutes until lightly golden. Brush with olive oil as soon as they come out of the oven and eat warm or cold.

Any leftover bread sticks can be stored in an airtight container or bread bin where they will stay fresh for 2–3 days. If you want to freeze the bread sticks, remove them from the oven 2–3 minutes before they are cooked and allow to cool, then seal in an airtight bag before freezing. Defrost the breadsticks and return to the oven for 3–4 minutes to finish cooking.

METHOD #9

ROTI

When we spent time in Nepal, we ate hundreds of these little flatbreads and learnt how to make them with the local tea shop owner. They are often served with curries and are excellent for mopping up a plate of dhal or spicy chutney. They are also eaten as a lunchtime snack and are delicious fried after cooking. The key to a successful roti is to roll it out thinly. This means that not only will it cook quickly and evenly, but it will also stay pliable enough to roll or bend round food. You can try adding herbs to the dough, but don't overdo it. There's a good reason why this recipe hasn't changed in thousands of years -- keeping it simple is the key.

PREPARING

Set up a floured work surface near the stove. This will allow you to roll out the next roti while you are keeping an eye on the first cooking in the pan. The first time you make roti you may prefer to roll out the whole batch and then cook them, but once you perfect the technique, you will enjoy the multi-tasking.

MAKING

The dough mix for this classic flatbread is extremely simple. Combine the wholemeal flour, tepid water and a generous pinch of salt in a bowl. Knead the dough for 5–10 minutes until smooth, then cover with a damp tea towel and leave to rest for 30 minutes. Divide the dough into balls and roll out as flat as you can. They should be 15–20cm (6–8 inches) across.

COOKING

Preheat a griddle or wok and test the temperature with the water test (see page 47). When the temperature is right, brush with oil, add a roti and cook for about 30 seconds on each side until lightly browned. Roti will sometimes puff up a bit and bubbles will appear on the surface, but don't worry if they don't.

The roti can be brushed with melted butter or ghee after cooking to add colour and make them pliable for longer, allowing for easier rolling and tearing.

STORING

Wrap the cooked roti in a tea towel while you cook the rest of the batch to keep them soft and pliable. They will become dry and leathery if you leave them uncovered.

If you want to freeze roti, slightly undercook them and allow to cool in a tea towel before sealing in a freezer bag. Defrost thoroughly and reheat on a greased griddle, or spray with a water mister, wrap in foil and reheat in a preheated oven at 180°C (350°F), Gas Mark 4, for 10 minutes.

HOW TO SHAPE AND COOK ROTI

1

2

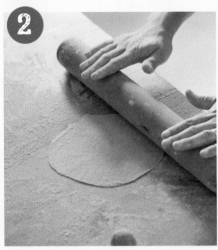

Knead the dough for 5–10 minutes. The gluten takes a while to develop elasticity so don't expect a particularly light and stretchy dough at the end. Cover and leave to rest for 30 minutes.

Divide the dough into 20–30g (¾–1¼oz) pieces. Roll out to 15cm (6 inch) rounds on a floured work surface, rotating the dough as you go for a uniform thickness and shape.

3

BASIC ROTI DOUGH

Makes 6–8

100g (3½oz) wholemeal flour, plus extra for dusting

a pinch of salt

60ml (2½fl oz) tepid water

oil, for brushing

Sift the flour and salt into a mixing bowl and add the water. Mix to form a dough. Then follow the instructions above to shape and cook a roti.

Heat a griddle and brush it with a little oil. Cook the rotis for 30 seconds each side until golden, then wrap in a tea towel while you cook the rest. Serve warm.

The greatest flatbread for creating a handy-sized wrap has to be the humble tortilla. Corn tortillas are thicker and more dense, perfect cut into segments and fried into crispy tortilla chips, or fried whole and used as a base for tostadas and tacos. The wheat tortilla is our favourite as it is more pliable to work with and tasty straight off the griddle.

MAKES 6-8

FOR THE TORTILLAS

250g (8oz) plain white flour
(or cornmeal for corn tortillas),
plus extra for dusting

a pinch of baking powder (optional)

5g (¼oz) salt

150ml (¼pint) tepid water

FOR THE QUESADILLAS

200g (7oz) Cheddar cheese, grated

24 jalapeño peppers, sliced

2 red onions, finely diced

2 tablespoons chopped fresh coriander

TO SERVE

soured cream (optional)

fresh tomato salsa

TEX-MEX QUESADILLAS

To make the dough for the tortillas, place all the ingredients in a mixing bowl and mix to a dough. Knead the dough for 5 minutes until smooth and elastic, then return to the bowl, cover and leave to rise for 30–40 minutes.

Divide the dough into 6–8 equal portions and roll out each on a floured work surface to a round about 2.5mm (⅛ inch) thick.

Preheat a griddle pan, check the temperature with the water test (see page 47), then cook the tortillas for 30 seconds on each side until golden brown. Wrap in a folded tea towel while you cook the remaining tortillas. They can be used immediately, or can be allowed to cool before filling.

To make the quesadillas, divide the filling ingredients between the tortillas, then fold in half to enclose the filling and press down. Reheat the griddle and cook the quesadillas for 2–3 minutes, turning once, until the cheese has melted. Cut into triangles and serve with soured cream, if liked, and fresh tomato salsa.

3

STARTERS

INTRODUCTION TO

STARTERS

A starter is the combination of natural yeast cultures and friendly lactic acid bacteria that develops when you provide flour with moisture and warmth, the conditions it needs to ferment. You then use this starter to make your bread dough -- simple. You could argue that using a starter is more complicated than using commercial yeast, but you have to weigh this up against the unique sour flavours, the wholesome chewy texture and the satisfaction of bread made completely at home!

WHY MAKE A STARTER?

A starter adds a natural yeasty flavour to bread and will help expand the types of grain that you can bake with, as a starter can be used to make rye bread rise, something commercial yeast cannot do. The best thing about keeping a culture of yeasts growing in your kitchen is that you won't ever need to nip to the shops to buy yeast if you feel the urge to bake.

Starters are convenient and can be adjusted with a couple of days notice for larger batches of bread. The other lovely thing about making your own starter is that you can give some to your friends and family.

AS IF BY MAGIC...

Water and warmth are essential for the yeasts and bacteria in the flour to grow. The whole process is one of symbiotic balance. Without getting too deep into the science, naturally occurring enzymes transform the carbohydrates in the flour into sugars to feed the yeast. There is a delicate chain of cooperation where the beneficial lactic acid bacteria help produce neutralizing antibiotics to prevent unwanted bacteria from ruining the sourdough.

The best thing about starters is that it all happens quickly, taking just 3–12 hours for the first signs to show. There will be bubbles and a distinctive smell. The smell develops as the culture matures and the yeast grows, becoming less harsh and more complex over the following days and weeks.

CONTAINERS

Begin by choosing an appropriate container with a lid for your starter. It needs to have lots of room to expand. Don't use a glass container with a tight-fitting lid unless you have no other option as the build-up of pressure can be significant. If you don't seal the lid, then a glass container could be suitable, but you may find a rather messy explosion of yeast if you aren't careful! We keep our starters in plastic tubs with lids as they are more flexible. A transparent container makes it easy to check on the bubbles without even having to move it. We also always label our starter and normally call it Mother or Mum.

REFRESHING OR FEEDING

This is the act of giving a starter more flour and water as it grows. The term 'feeding' is misleading because, in fact, you are not just

Twist from the wrist as you score your loaf

Once proved, transfer your dough to a dusted baking peel

providing nourishment for the initial yeast. The fresh flour contains more yeasts and bacteria, so we prefer the term 'refreshing' when adding more flour and water to the starter. The terms are interchangeable, but it's good to understand the magic of what's going on in the culture.

To begin with, you will find that refreshing your starter is a daily activity and after your starter is established, if you are baking regularly, it may continue and become part of your daily routine. Don't let this commitment put you off trying a starter as it really is very simple and doesn't take long. Keep the starter at room temperature and whisk in fresh flour and water each day, or store it in the refrigerator and it can go for a week without refreshing.

RIPE & READY TO BAKE

Knowing when a starter is ready to bake is a bit like knowing when a volcano is ready to erupt. You know because it is vigorous and bubbly. An expert baker may offer exact seismic readings but we feel that it is about observing the way it looks and making a cautious judgement. If you leave it too long, the yeasts will start to exhaust themselves and growth will slow down again until the starter is refreshed with more flour and water. The best advice is to look at the container and see when the lid is bulging and the surface of the starter is covered with a film of small bubbles like soap lather.

If you want to time the ripening for a bake, take the starter out of the refrigerator, refresh it and leave in a warm place like an airing cupboard for 12–24 hours. This will almost definitely give you a ripe starter to bake with. The riper the starter, the better the bread will become. Active yeasts and bacteria can radically improve the gluten in the dough and create a delicious bread.

THE RIGHT CONSISTENCY

Many bakers recommend adding more flour than water and keeping a stiff starter in the refrigerator. This is down to personal choice. The benefit of a stiff starter is that the signs of ripeness are easier to spot. If it is bulging into an aerated dome, you're ready to bake; if it has collapsed then it is too young or has gone over. The disadvantage is that every time you refresh the dough, you'll have to get your hands dirty and knead it. We're obviously not precious about working with our hands, but there are advantages to keeping a wetter starter as you can simply whisk in the flour and water and get on with the rest of your day.

CHOOSING YOUR GRAIN

Natural yeasts and lactic acid bacteria are present in many grains that are used to make flour. The best choice for a simple starter is rye, but wheat and spelt flours can be used too. A wheat starter will be slightly more lively than a starter made with rye flour. If you are unable to keep an eye on its progress, you may want to add less water and more flour to give a stiffer starter as it will be slower to develop, therefore reducing the risk of it going over or fermenting too quickly and exhausting the supply of food for the yeast.

To make a spelt starter, we'd recommend taking a shortcut and using some rye starter to give it a head start. Instead of starting from scratch, simply combine 25g (1oz) of established rye starter with 100g (3½oz) of spelt flour and 75ml (3fl oz) of water. Then keep the mixture going by refreshing with spelt flour instead of rye flour.

STORING

You can store your starter at room temperature, in the refrigerator or freezer. Freezing is ideal if you want to have a back-up batch. This is a good safety net in case something happens to your starter or if you can't find anyone to look after it when you go away on holiday!

If you've got too much starter, give some away to friends. In many countries there are strong traditions of passing down sourdough cultures through generations and they can be kept alive for a lifetime. Share a cupful in a plastic tub or add some extra flour, knead into a dough and hand over a bag to your friends and family.

HOW LONG UNTIL NEXT BAKE?	WHERE TO STORE YOUR STARTER
0–3 days	Room temperature; ideally 28–30°C (82–86°F) (daily refreshment to ripen ready for baking)
3–30 days	Refrigerator at 5°C (41°F) (weekly refreshment)
30–60 days	Freezer

SOURDOUGH

The technique of rising bread with natural yeasts is thousands of years old
and surprisingly easy. You may fear that maintaining a culture of wild yeasts
is going to be demanding and worry about becoming a slave to some sour-smelling
monster. The reality is that developing your own sourdough starter is far simpler
than looking after a pet goldfish. Forget about any advice to use raisins, milk,
grapes or yoghurt to provide the yeasts. The simplest and shortest route to a
sustainable sourdough is flour and water. There really is no nonsense, just
a bit of patience and attentive refreshing.

PREPARING

To make your own sourdough, you will need
a warm place to store the starter. Between
28°C (82°F) and 30°C (86°F) is perfect, but
a few degrees either side and you're unlikely
to kill your yeast but it will slow down the
process. Try placing it close to a radiator or
a wood-burner, in an airing cupboard or a
standard plant propagator – just remember
to check the temperature before placing your
starter in its new home.

MAKING THE STARTER

Mix the flour and water to a paste in your
chosen container (see page 60) and sprinkle
a little extra flour over the top to prevent
the water from evaporating and to form an
extra barrier or protective skin. Cover with
a lid or clingfilm. After 24 hours, whisk in
more flour and water and return the starter
to a warm place.

The next day you should find that the starter
has begun to change. It should show signs
of frothing with small bubbles covering the
surface. The smell may also have started to
become quite potent. It may take a few days

or weeks for the starter to develop a
distinctive flavour of its own, but for now
it should smell acidic like rotten apples.

Often the sourdough starter will separate
while it is maturing. If you see a grey liquid
on the surface, simply whisk it in the next
time you refresh the mixture. Continue
adding more flour and water each day
until the starter is ready to use (see page 62).
A ripe sourdough starter will be active and
full of little bubbles.

MAKING THE BREAD

To allow the sourdough starter plenty of time to ripen, mix in the flour and water the night before baking. This is called making a sponge and it helps create a bread with a good crust and plenty of random air holes inside.

The next day, combine the sponge with the dough ingredients and knead until elastic. Cover, leave to rise for an hour, then knock back, shape and prove in a basket or loaf tin.

COOKING

Bake the dough in a very hot oven for the first 10–15 minutes to form a crust, then turn down the temperature and continue baking until the sourdough is starting to turn golden brown. See pages 66–7 for more details.

STORING

Leave for 12–24 hours before eating to allow the bread to firm up and the flavour to develop, then store any leftover bread in a bread bin or wrapped in greaseproof paper or clingfilm where it will stay fresh for 4–5 days.

SIMPLE SOURDOUGH

Makes 2 large loaves

FOR THE SOURDOUGH STARTER
200g (7oz) wholemeal rye flour
200ml (7fl oz) tepid water

FOR THE SPONGE
150g (5oz) sourdough starter (from above)
200g (7oz) strong white flour
100ml (3½fl oz) tepid water

FOR THE DOUGH
400g (13oz) strong white flour
200ml (7fl oz) tepid water
10g (⅜oz) salt

To make this bread, follow the instructions opposite and on pages 66–7.

HOW TO MAKE SOURDOUGH

Mix 50g (2oz) of wholemeal rye flour in a bowl with 50ml (2fl oz) of tepid water. Use a whisk or wooden spoon to mix well, cover and leave in a warm place for 24 hours.

Stir in another 50g (2oz) of flour and 50ml (2fl oz) of tepid water. Cover and return to a warm place for 24 hours.

To make the sponge, mix 150g (5oz) of the starter in a bowl with 200g (7oz) of strong white flour and 100ml (3½fl oz) of tepid water. Cover and leave to rest overnight.

Mix the sponge with the dough ingredients, knead for 10 minutes until elastic, cover and leave to rise for 1 hour. Knock back, shape into 2 balls and place seam side up in proving baskets.

Add another 50g (2oz) of flour and 50ml (2fl oz) of tepid water and stir in any greyish liquid. Cover and return to a warm place for 24 hours.

By day 4 the starter should now be frothing nicely and taste mildly acidic. Add another batch of flour and tepid water and leave to ripen for 12–24 hours.

Cover and leave to prove for 3–4 hours. Test the readiness by gently pressing your finger into the dough. It is ready to go in the oven when the indentation disappears fairly slowly.

Transfer the dough to a baking peel or greased baking sheet. Slash the top of the loaves and bake at 220°C (425°F), Gas Mark 7, for 10 minutes, then 200°C (400°F), Gas Mark 6, for 40 minutes.

We have been in love with bruschetta since a family holiday to Rome and now quickly prepare it every summer as a great way to use up our gluts of home-grown seasonal vegetables. Bruschetta is wonderful made with sourdough bread, but is also delicious with ciabatta (see page 80).

SERVES 6-8

1 small to medium white sourdough loaf, sliced
2-4 garlic cloves, peeled
salt and freshly ground black pepper
olive oil, for drizzling (optional)

FOR THE COURGETTE TOPPING

2 small courgettes
juice of ½ a lemon
1 teaspoon chopped fresh oregano
1 tablespoon olive oil

FOR THE TOMATO & BASIL TOPPING

3-4 ripe tomatoes, diced
12 fresh basil leaves, roughly torn
1 tablespoon olive oil

FOR THE FUNGHI TOPPING

1 tablespoon olive oil
100g (3½oz) mushrooms, chopped
1 teaspoon chopped fresh parsley

BRUSCHETTA TRIO

To make the courgette topping, slice the courgettes into long ribbons using a vegetable peeler, then cook on a preheated hot griddle until just tender. Transfer to a bowl, add the remaining ingredients and toss to combine.

To make the tomato and basil topping, mix together the ingredients in a small bowl.

To make the funghi topping, heat the oil in a frying pan, add the mushrooms and fry until golden, then add the parsley.

Preheat the grill to high and toast the bread on both sides. Rub the garlic cloves over both sides of the slices so they grate themselves on the rough toast. Top the bruschetta with the toppings, season with a little salt and pepper and drizzle with more olive oil, if necessary.

A beef sandwich made with horseradish sourdough becomes greater than the sum of its parts. The ingrained heat from the bread provides the perfect background for the juicy slices of rare beef and peppery watercress.

SERVES 4

FOR THE HORSERADISH SOURDOUGH
100g (3½oz) sourdough starter (see pages 65-7)

500g (1lb) strong white flour

250ml (8fl oz) tepid water

10g (⅜oz) salt

50g (2oz) butter, softened

1 tablespoon finely grated horseradish

1 teaspoon chopped fresh thyme

FOR THE SANDWICHES
300g (10oz) beef fillet

1 tablespoon olive oil

salt and freshly ground black pepper

softened butter, for spreading

4 handfuls of watercress

BEEF & HORSERADISH SOURDOUGH OPEN SANDWICH

Activate the sourdough starter by refreshing it the night before and keeping in a warmer place overnight (see pages 62–3). Combine it with the flour, water and salt to make a dough and knead for 10 minutes until smooth and elastic. Flatten the dough and spread the softened butter over the top, then knead again until evenly distributed. Repeat with the horseradish and thyme.

Cover and leave to rise for 4–5 hours, stretching the dough and folding it in on itself every hour or so. Knock back and shape the dough, then transfer to a proving basket and leave to prove, covered, for 3 hours.

Preheat the oven to 220°C (425°F), Gas Mark 7, and grease a baking sheet. Transfer the dough to the prepared baking sheet, slash the top, mist with water and cook in the oven for 45–50 minutes, reducing the oven temperature to 200°C (400°F), Gas Mark 6, after 10 minutes. Remove from the oven and allow the bread to cool. Leave for 12–24 hours before eating to allow the bread to firm up and the flavour to develop.

Brush the piece of beef fillet on all sides with the oil, then season generously. Cook on a preheated hot ridged griddle for 3–4 minutes, turning regularly, then transfer to a plate. The beef should be rare in the middle. Cover loosely with foil and leave to rest for 10–15 minutes.

Carve the beef thinly and slice the bread. Butter the bread and top each slice with the warm beef carpaccio. Serve immediately with a side portion of watercress.

Store any leftover bread in a bread bin or wrapped in greaseproof paper or clingfilm where it will stay fresh for 4–5 days.

This loaf is fragrant, sweet and lightly spiced. The dates give it a satisfying chewy quality and the aroma is rich and exotic. Some people enjoy sweet breads like this with savoury meals, but they are most popular as teabreads, served with a hot brew and a slab of butter.

MAKES 1 LARGE LOAF

100g (3½oz) sourdough starter
(see pages 65–7)

250g (8oz) wholemeal flour

200g (7oz) rye flour

300ml (10fl oz) tepid water

10g (⅜oz) salt

50g (2oz) dates, chopped

50g (2oz) pecan nuts, crushed

1 tablespoon dried rosemary, crushed

½ teaspoon ground star anise
or cinnamon

oil, for greasing

TO SERVE

butter

honey

DATE & PECAN SOURDOUGH

Activate the sourdough starter by refreshing it the night before and keeping in a warmer place overnight (see pages 62–3). Combine it with the wholemeal and rye flours, water and salt to make a dough and knead for 10 minutes. Near the end of the kneading time, combine the remaining ingredients into the dough and knead well to distribute evenly. Cover and leave to rise for 3–4 hours.

Knock back and shape the dough into a ball, then transfer to a proving basket and leave to prove, covered, for 3 hours.

Preheat the oven to 220°C (425°F), Gas Mark 7, and grease a baking sheet. Transfer the dough to the prepared baking sheet and slash the top. Generously spray inside the oven with a water mister, then cook the bread in the oven for 10 minutes. Reduce the temperature to 200°C (400°F), Gas Mark 6, and cook for a further 40 minutes. Remove from the oven and allow the bread to cool. Leave for 12–24 hours before eating to allow the bread to firm up and the flavour to develop. Serve sliced and toasted with cold butter and golden honey.

Store any leftover bread in a bread bin or wrapped in greaseproof paper or clingfilm where it will stay fresh for 5–7 days.

BARM

The perfect rustic loaf

Barm is an old way of making bread using the yeast found in ale. The process is very similar to sourdough and our quick method actually involves using a spoonful of our sourdough starter to kick-start the process. The key to success is using a bottle of beer with live yeast in it, heating the beer to the right temperature and leaving the barm to ferment until it's really frothy. Barm is delicious served with pea and ham soup.

PREPARING

First select a good local beer. The beer must be bottle-conditioned so there is still live yeast active within it. Then you will need to make a barm starter by mixing the beer with flour and some sourdough starter. We use some of our established sourdough starter but you could make your own from scratch using water and strong white flour (see pages 65–7).

MAKING

Make the dough by combining the barm starter with the flour, water and salt and kneading for 2 minutes. Leave to rest for 10 minutes, then knead again for 30 seconds and repeat twice. Now knead for 30 seconds every hour for 4–5 hours. Shape the dough and transfer to a proving basket. Cover and leave to prove for 3–4 hours.

COOKING

Turn the dough on to a greased baking sheet or preheated baking stone and cook in a preheated oven at 220°C (425°F), Gas Mark 7, for 40–50 minutes.

STORING

Leave for 12–24 hours before eating to allow the bread to firm up and the flavour to develop, then store any leftover bread in a bread bin or wrapped in greaseproof paper or clingfilm where it will stay fresh for 4–5 days.

BASIC BARM

Makes 1 large or 2 small loaves

FOR THE BARM STARTER

250ml (8fl oz) bottle-conditioned beer

50g (2oz) strong white flour

2 tablespoons sourdough starter (see pages 65–7)

FOR THE DOUGH

150g (5oz) barm starter (from above)

500g (1lb) strong white flour

200ml (7fl oz) tepid water

10g (³/₈oz) salt

To make this bread, follow the instructions above and opposite.

HOW TO MAKE BARM

To make the barm starter, heat the beer to 70°C (158°F) and stir in the flour. Cool to room temperature, then add the sourdough starter. Cover and leave overnight to ferment.

Combine 150g (5oz) of the barm starter with the remaining dough ingredients and work to a smooth dough. Leave to rest for 10 minutes.

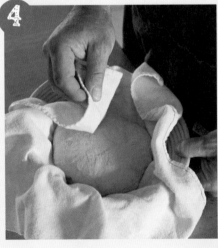

Knead the dough for 30 seconds, then rest for 10 minutes and repeat twice. Now reduce the frequency of kneading to once every hour and continue for 4–5 hours.

Shape the dough and leave to prove for 3–4 hours. It is ready to bake when almost doubled in size. Bake at 220°C (425°F), Gas Mark 7, for 40–50 minutes.

This is our twist on a traditional way of eating stew, where the bread is the bowl. The barm bread complements this rustic stew nicely, and the rich beer gravy bread slowly softens the bread 'bowl' once the stew has been served. This is a great dish for a cold winter evening.

MAKES 4

1 quantity Basic Barm dough
(see pages 74-5)

oil, for greasing

100g (3½oz) butter

500g (11b) shoulder of lamb, diced

2 red onions, diced

2 parsnips, diced

2 carrots, diced

½ a swede, diced

4 sprigs of fresh rosemary, chopped

3 tablespoons plain flour

1.2 litres (2 pints) Guinness or stout

250ml (8fl oz) water

salt and freshly ground black pepper

BREAD BOWL STEW

Make the barm dough and leave to rise for 4–5 hours, kneading lightly at intervals, following the instructions on page 75. Divide the dough into 4, shape into round loaves and leave to prove in proving baskets. Transfer to a baking sheet and cook following the instructions on page 75. Once cooled, cut the tops off the cooked loaves with a bread knife and scoop out a little dough to make a bowl shape inside each loaf.

Alternatively, make the bread bowls by dividing the dough into 4 balls.and rolling out the dough on a lightly floured work surface to make 4 rounds, 12–15cm (5–6 inches) in diameter. Grease the undersides of 4 ovenproof soup bowls and place them upside down on a baking sheet. Lay the rounds of dough over the upturned bowls and smooth out to expel any air pockets between the dough and the bowls. Cover and leave to prove in a warm place for 1 hour. Preheat the oven to 220°C (425°F), Gas Mark 7. Cook the bread in the oven for 10 minutes, then reduce the temperature to 200°C (400°F), Gas Mark 6, and cook for a further 20 minutes. Remove from the bowls and allow to cool on a wire rack for at least 30 minutes.

To make the stew, melt the butter in a heavy-based pan over a high heat and brown the meat on all sides. Add the diced vegetables and herbs and cook for about 3 minutes, then add the flour, stir well to combine and cook for 2 minutes. Add the Guinness and water. Season to taste, bring to the boil, then reduce the heat and simmer for 1–2 hours until the meat and vegetables are tender.

Divide the stew between the bread bowls and serve.

PUMPERNICKEL

Pumpernickel is a traditional German bread that is dense, dark and highly textured. It takes a long time to make and bake -- hence the almost black colour -- but the delicious result will be a worthy reward for your patience.

PREPARING

The night before you want to make the pumpernickel, mix together the starter in one bowl and the soaker in another. Place the starter in a warm place to ferment; this adds flavour and maturity to the dough, vital when using a heavy grain like rye with little gluten structure.

MAKING

To make the dough the following day, pass the soaker through a sieve and retain the liquid. The bread and rye berries can be fed to chickens or discarded. Warm the soaking liquid until tepid and mix with the starter and dough ingredients. Use your hand like a claw rather than in a kneading motion as no amount of work will improve the elasticity of this dough. Once the dough is smooth, put in a loaf tin and place in a warm place for 3–4 hours to rest.

COOKING

Cover the bread with foil or a lid before it goes in the oven. Pumpernickel needs steam to cook, so place a roasting tin in the bottom of the oven and keep it topped up with about 2.5cm (1 inch) of water during cooking. Start with the oven at 200°C (400°F), Gas Mark 6, and reduce the temperature every hour by 10°C (25°F), 1 Gas Mark, cooking it at 150°C (300°F), Gas Mark 2, for the final hour. Turn off the oven and allow the bread to cool inside.

STORING

Once cool, wrap in greaseproof paper and leave to mature for a day before eating. Pumpernickel will keep for about 1–2 weeks. To preserve it for a long period, keep in a sealed zip-lock bag or pack with a vacuum packer.

PUMPERNICKEL

Makes 1 loaf

FOR THE STARTER

300g (10oz) rye flour

300ml (½ pint) tepid water

50g (2oz) sourdough starter
(see pages 65–7)

FOR THE SOAKER

200g (7oz) rye berries

200g (7oz) rye bread or stale
brown bread, sliced

450ml (¾ pint) water

FOR THE DOUGH

250g (8oz) rye flour

250g (8oz) rye flakes

50g (2oz) molasses

20g (¾oz) salt

To make this bread, follow the instructions above and opposite.

HOW TO MAKE PUMPERNICKEL

Mix the starter ingredients in one bowl, and the soaker ingredients in another bowl. Cover and leave overnight. Stir the soaker from time to time and submerge the floating bits.

The next morning, strain the bread and berries. Transfer 300ml (½ pint) of the soaking liquid to a pan, making up the quantity with water if necessary, and heat until tepid.

Mix the soaking liquid with the fermented starter and the dough ingredients and stir well with your hands. Scoop into a greased loaf tin and leave to rest for 3–4 hours.

Cook at 200°C (400°F), Gas Mark 6, for 1 hour. Reduce the temperature every hour for 5 hours in total, until it is at 150°C (300°F), Gas Mark 2, for the final hour. Cool in the oven.

METHOD #13

CIABATTA

Ciabatta is the perfect bread for a lunchtime panini, or tearing while still warm and dipping in oil and balsamic vinegar. In Italy it is known as 'slipper' bread due to the elongated shape it forms when you stretch it before it goes into the oven. Ciabatta is made using a starter, but the starter can be made with commercial yeast rather than a sourdough culture, so it is very easy to make.

PREPARING

Prepare the starter well in advance. It helps the dough to become active and light and adds a great flavour. Let the starter rest overnight or up to 24 hours before using, keeping it covered with a damp tea towel or clingfilm, or placing the bowl in a sealed bin bag.

MAKING

Mix the starter with the combined dough ingredients and work for 10 minutes. Ciabatta dough is soft, wet and sticky, so keep a pile of semolina flour or cornflour for dusting close at hand. Normal kneading techniques may not work to begin with, so try forming your hand into a claw and mix until smooth, then turn out on to a floured work surface and knead until elastic. Return to the greased bowl, drizzle with more oil and leave to rise.

When the dough is light and airy, turn it on to a floured surface and gently press down, spreading it into a rectangle by using your fingers to dimple the surface rather than stretching the dough. Flour the top again and cut into equal pieces. Fold the 2 ends of the loaves into the middle, then fold in the long sides. Turn over and place on a greased baking sheet or floured tea towel and leave to prove.

COOKING

Dust the loaves well with semolina flour just before baking, then give the dough a final stretch by holding both ends and gently elongating the middle. Preheat the oven to 220°C (425°F), Gas Mark 7, and spray the inside with a water mister before putting the bread in, to create lots of steam. Cook the bread for about 20 minutes until golden, then cool on a wire rack.

STORING

Any leftover ciabatta can be stored in a plastic bag or wrapped in greaseproof paper where it will stay fresh for 2–3 days. Alternatively, store in the freezer for 2–3 months.

NOW TRY: AVOCADO CIABATTA

Use avocado oil instead of olive oil to make the dough. This delicate oil adds a fresh vibrant taste without overpowering the yeasty aroma.

CIABATTA

Makes 4 loaves

FOR THE STARTER

200g (7oz) strong white flour

200ml (7fl oz) tepid water

5g (¼oz) fresh yeast, crumbled

FOR THE DOUGH

10g (⅜oz) fresh yeast

450g (14½oz) strong white flour
or 00 flour

15g (½oz) salt

325ml (11fl oz) tepid water

50ml (2fl oz) olive oil

semolina flour or cornflour,
for dusting

To make this bread, follow the instructions
below and opposite.

HOW TO MAKE CIABATTA

Make the starter by stirring together the
ingredients thoroughly in a bowl. Whisk or
work to remove any lumps. Cover and leave
in a warm place for 12–24 hours.

To make the dough, rub the yeast into the
flour, add the salt, water and oil and mix well.
Add the starter and knead for 10 minutes.
Return to the greased bowl and leave to rise
for 1–2 hours.

Cut the dough into 4 rectangles and fold in
the edges to form neat loaves. Place seam
side down on a greased baking sheet and dust
with semolina flour. Prove for 45 minutes
before baking.

This traditional peasant dish transforms stale bread into a succulent summer meal. The bread in the Tuscan version can be rather soggy, which is not to everyone's taste, so we crisp up the bread in the oven before tossing it in the dressing. Our version of this Italian classic includes less traditional ingredients, such as melon balls, chunks of Gorgonzola, strips of air-dried ham and fresh mint.

SERVES 4

500g (1lb) stale ciabatta or sourdough bread, cut into chunks

2 tablespoons olive oil

3 ripe tomatoes, thickly sliced

½ cucumber, thickly sliced

1 red onion, cut into rough segments

½ a small melon, diced or balled

100g (3½oz) Gorgonzola cheese, diced

6 slices of air-dried ham, finely sliced

2 tablespoons capers

12 fresh mint leaves

FOR THE DRESSING

5 tablespoons olive oil

3 tablespoons red wine vinegar

1 teaspoon caster sugar

salt and freshly ground black pepper

PANZANELLA

Preheat the oven to 200°C (400°F), Gas Mark 6. Place the chunks of bread on a baking sheet, drizzle with the olive oil and cook in the oven for about 10 minutes, tossing in the oil from time to time, until crisp and golden.

Transfer the bread to a large serving bowl and add the tomatoes, cucumber, onion, melon, cheese, ham and capers. Whisk together the dressing ingredients in a small bowl, season to taste and pour over the salad. Toss well, cover and chill in the refrigerator for 1 hour, if time permits.

Bring the salad back to room temperature, add the mint leaves and toss the salad again to coat all the ingredients in the dressing. Check and adjust the seasoning if necessary and serve at room temperature.

4

YEASTS

INTRODUCTION TO
YEASTS

It is easy to say what you like about a good slice of bread, and equally what you don't like. It may be beautiful and light, punctuated with bubbles of fresh aroma, or it might be heavy, dense and chewy. It could have a golden crust that crackles and crunches when you bite, or it could be pale and soft. If you have baked this bread yourself, your feelings are much more intense. A loaf of bread that works according to plan is truly enjoyable, but a bread that doesn't come up to scratch is subjected to severe criticism, reflection and thoughts of improvement. Yeast-risen breads are perhaps most familiar to us, and when you bake a bread you've been eating all your life, the pressure is really on.

WORKING WITH YEAST

When baking yeast-risen breads, the key is to look after the yeast and nurture it throughout the process. The standard procedure, outlined on pages 20–37, explains all you need to understand about dealing with yeast and making these breads, so refresh your knowledge of the principles before you begin trying out the recipes in this chapter.

BASIC BREAD

Once you have mastered the basic flour to water ratios and techniques for baking white bread, the recipe will be part of your skill-set forever. We adapt and experiment with types of flour, flavours, coatings and shapes, but the basic recipe remains unchanged. You will find slight inconsistencies when using different flour – some grains will retain slightly more water, take more working or offer greater texture.

FLAVOURED BREADS

Often bread is regarded as the side show of a meal or as a warm-up act. It is served in a basket or used purely to hold a filling rather than as meal in itself. Flavouring a basic yeast dough with other ingredients is an excellent way to bring it centre stage, and also offers the opportunity of adding more vitamins and minerals to your bread.

Flavoured breads, such as Beetroot Bread (see page 108), can look radically different to a basic loaf and we believe anything that excites the eyes also excites the tastebuds. A colourful slice of bread adds variety to the routine of baking and allows you to become extremely experimental. Baking is not generally open to experimentation and the method of producing the right conditions for a yeast dough to rise and develop structure remain constant. This is why an exciting addition to your dough can free you creatively and make baking even more fun.

SHAPED LOAVES & ROLLS

When children around the world are asked to draw a loaf of bread, it won't always look like it has come out of a loaf tin. The sheer choice of different shapes and sizes is what makes baking so enticing. Whenever we have

Egg wash is the gold leaf of the baking world

Make time to enjoy the rewards of baking

been lucky enough to travel, we have been fascinated by the different ways people shape bread. Some are highly decorative, others practical or traditional, but all of them are worth trying at home at least once.

Yeast enables bread to rise and a strong gluten structure opens up the potential to shape bread into all sorts of forms. Don't be afraid to treat your dough like putty and practise making a range of shapes until you are comfortable with them.

Arrange baguettes and rolls on a floured cloth to prove so that they don't stick together as they expand. Folding the fabric creates partitions that give your bread the right shape to prove in. Once you've mastered a selection of different shapes, move on to the more exotic and artisan breads. The disadvantage of shaping bread into different forms is that it takes longer. We save the more unusual breads like bagels, crumpets and muffins for special occasions. Make time to try them and you won't be disappointed.

BUTTER-ENRICHED BREADS

Adding butter to dough will create a lovely rich loaf, and the extra fat will help the bread to last. The first time that you work a dough that includes butter you will find it unusual, but persevere because it's worth it. The velvety dough will be more orange than normal and taste incredible.

OLIVE OIL BREADS

Fat helps to keep bread for longer; our favourite way to extend the shelf-life and taste of bread is incorporating oil. Olive oil is used in many Mediterranean breads and adds elasticity and colour to the dough. If you want to bake really tasty pizza or focaccia, invest in good-quality olive oil. We use a mid-range extra virgin olive oil. It seems wrong pouring a very expensive oil into dough, so we pour it into a bowl and dip the fresh bread into it. Olive oil breads are perfect for vegans as they contain no dairy products.

SWEET BREADS

It is surprising how one food can be adjusted in so many ways to fit into every part of your daily life. Bread can be served as a dessert if you use sugar, fruit and spices in the dough. Neither of us has a particularly sweet tooth, but the balance of texture and flavour in bread recipes like stollen (see page 148) and brioche (see page 138) are difficult for a cake to surpass. We have found over the years that there are certain combinations that work magic with a batch of dough. Dusting with cinnamon and icing sugar instead of flour sounds like a simple substitution but it shouldn't be under-rated. The difficulty with sweet breads is to find that fine balance between the fruit, spices or nuts so that you don't just end up with a lump of sweet dough that has no depth.

The same methods are used to create sweet breads as savoury breads, but some require extra kit, such as a deep-fat fryer for making doughnuts. You may also like to invest in some baking tins in different shapes if you are serious.

COOKING WITH BREAD

There are hundreds of recipes that use bread as an ingredient. Often these involve breadcrumbs but there are many more inspiring ways to use bread in your cooking. We've found that our repertoire of bread-based recipes has grown over the years in parallel with our love of baking.

If you are going to try baking just one loaf of bread at home, then this has to be a contender. It is simply a classic and perfect for a sandwich or toast. When you take a loaf of white bread out of the oven, the nostalgic effect and the feel-good factor are hard to beat.

MAKES 1 LARGE OR 2 SMALL LOAVES

500g (1lb) strong white flour,
plus extra for dusting

10g (⅜oz) fresh yeast

10g (⅜oz) salt

350ml (12fl oz) tepid water

oil, for greasing

WHITE LOAF

To make the dough, place the flour in a mixing bowl and crumble in the yeast. Rub the yeast into the flour with the fingertips until the mixture resembles fine breadcrumbs. Stir in the salt, then pour in the water and mix to a dough.

Knead the dough for 8–10 minutes until smooth and elastic, then return to the bowl, cover and leave to rise in a warm place for 1–2 hours.

Lightly grease 1 large or 2 small loaf tins. Transfer the dough to a lightly floured work surface, knock back and divide into 2 pieces if using 2 tins. Shape each piece into an oval, flattening gently with your fingertips, then fold the ends into the middle and roll to form a sausage shape about two-thirds of the length of the tin(s). Place the dough seam side down in the tin(s), cover and leave to prove in a warm place for 45 minutes, or until the dough has doubled in size and is just up to the rim.

Preheat the oven to 220°C (425°F), Gas Mark 7, and cook small loaves for 25–30 minutes or large loaves for 40–50 minutes, reducing the oven temperature to 200°C (400°F), Gas Mark 6, after 10 minutes. Turn the loaves out of the tins and return to the oven for a further 5 minutes if you want the base to have a firmer crust. Allow to cool on a wire rack.

Any leftover bread can be stored in a plastic bag or wrapped in greaseproof paper where it will stay fresh for 2–3 days. Alternatively, store in the freezer for 2–3 months, having sliced the bread first so you can defrost only what you need.

It is often more enjoyable to eat simple, healthy food with a guilt-free conscience than devour a slice of some gourmet treat. Wholemeal flour does exactly this for bread! Serve with butter and honey or homemade marmalade.

MAKES 1 LARGE OR 2 SMALL LOAVES

600g (1lb 3½oz) strong wholemeal flour, plus extra for dusting

10g (⅜oz) fresh yeast

10g (⅜oz) salt

400ml (14fl oz) tepid water

oil, for greasing

1 tablespoon oat flakes

WHOLEMEAL LOAF

To make the dough, place the flour in a mixing bowl and crumble in the yeast. Rub the yeast into the flour with the fingertips until the mixture resembles fine breadcrumbs. Stir in the salt, then pour in the water and mix to a dough.

Don't worry if the dough seems wetter than normal: the extra water will be absorbed as the gluten structure develops. Avoid incorporating too much extra flour. Knead the dough for 10 minutes until smooth and elastic, then return to the bowl, cover and leave to rise in a warm place for 2 hours.

Lightly grease 1 or 2 baking sheets. Transfer the dough to a lightly floured work surface, knock back and divide into 2 pieces if making 2 loaves. Shape each piece into a round loaf (see page 27). Place the dough on the sheet(s), spray the surface with a water mister and sprinkle with the oat flakes. Cover and leave to prove in a warm place for 45 minutes, or until the dough has doubled in size.

Preheat the oven to 230°C (450°F), Gas Mark 8, and cook small loaves for 30–40 minutes or large loaves for 35–45 minutes, reducing the oven temperature to 200°C (400°F), Gas Mark 6, after 10 minutes. Turn the loaves out of the tins and return to the oven for a further 5 minutes if you want the base to have a firmer crust. Allow to cool on a wire rack.

Any leftover bread can be stored in a plastic bag or wrapped in greaseproof paper where it will stay fresh for 2–3 days. Alternatively, store in the freezer for 2–3 months, having sliced the bread first so you can defrost only what you need.

This recipe has kept us happy for many years and is superb served with smoked mackerel pâté and chutney, or for a sweeter slice with a drizzle of honey. The larger seeds add texture inside the dough and the all-over coating gives the crust an enticing appearance. Use lard instead of olive oil if you'd like to store the bread for longer.

MAKES 3 SMALL LOAVES

450g (14½oz) strong wholemeal flour

200g (7oz) strong white flour, plus extra for dusting

15g (½oz) fresh yeast

10g (³⁄₈oz) salt

325ml (11fl oz) tepid water

2 tablespoons sunflower seeds

2 tablespoons pumpkin seeds

1 tablespoon olive oil or 15g (½oz) lard, plus extra for greasing

2 tablespoons mixed seeds (linseeds, sesame, poppy or hemp)

GRANNY'S MULTI-SEED LOAF

To make the dough, place the wholemeal and white flours in a mixing bowl and crumble in the yeast. Rub the yeast into the flour with the fingertips until the mixture resembles fine breadcrumbs. Stir in the salt, then pour in the water and mix to a dough.

Knead the dough for 8–10 minutes until smooth and elastic, then sprinkle the sunflower seeds and pumpkin seeds on top and knead briefly until evenly distributed. Return to the bowl, cover and leave to rise in a warm place for 1 hour. The dough should rise to at least twice its original size.

Lightly grease 3 small loaf tins. Transfer the dough to a lightly floured work surface, knock back and knead briefly, then divide into 3 pieces. Shape each piece into a tight oval. Spread the mixed seeds on a plate and roll the dough in them to cover. Place the dough seam side down in the tins, cover and leave to prove in a warm place for 45 minutes.

Preheat the oven to 230°C (450°F), Gas Mark 8, and cook the bread for 10 minutes, then reduce the temperature to 200°C (400°F), Gas Mark 6, and cook for a further 15 minutes. Turn the loaves out of the tins and allow to cool on a wire rack.

Any leftover bread can be stored in a plastic bag or wrapped in greaseproof paper where it will stay fresh for 2–3 days. Alternatively, store in the freezer for 2–3 months, having sliced the bread first so you can defrost only what you need.

Some old-fashioned puddings have stood the test of time not because they are a special family tradition but because they still taste absolutely fantastic. This summer pudding captures the fruity delights of a season and morphs stale bread into a decadent treat.

SERVES 6

100g (3½oz) blackberries, plus extra to decorate

150g (5oz) redcurrants, stalks removed

500g (11b) raspberries, plus extra to decorate

150g (5oz) caster sugar

2 tablespoons elderflower or blackcurrant cordial

about 8 thick slices of slightly stale white bread, crusts removed

double cream, to serve

SUMMER BERRY PUDDING

Place all the fruit in a pan and sprinkle with the sugar. Set aside for 1–2 hours to draw out the juice, then add the cordial. Place over a medium heat and bring to the boil, then reduce the heat and simmer for 10–15 minutes. Allow to cool.

Choose a pudding basin or deep bowl which will hold the fruit. Cut a round of bread to fit the base of the basin and put in place. Line the sides of the basin with strips of bread arranged vertically and butted up close together, then pour the fruit into the centre.

Arrange a layer of bread on top of the fruit to enclose it completely, then cover with a plate slightly smaller in diameter than the rim of the basin. Place the basin on a tray to catch any escaping juice and weigh down the plate with some bags of rice or cans. Refrigerate overnight.

To turn out the pudding, remove the plate and weights and slide a palette knife down the edges between the bread and the basin. Place a deep serving plate, upside down, on top of the basin and hold firmly in place as you turn the basin and plate over and shake carefully to release the pudding on to the plate. Arrange some fresh blackberries and raspberries around the outside of the pudding. Cut into wedges and serve with double cream.

This is a twist on the sweet classic that is usually served as a dessert. Instead of using a custard to bind the bread pudding together, we are substituting it with a herby white wine sauce and plenty of finely chopped leeks. The lemon zest and pepper help to cut through the creamy elements and give the whole thing a balanced flavour. Serve with sausages, roast chicken or thick slices of gammon.

SERVES 4-6

1 small loaf of white bread

50g (2oz) butter, plus extra for greasing

1-2 leeks, finely sliced

50ml (2fl oz) white wine or water

3 large eggs

650ml (1 pint 2fl oz) milk

a pinch of grated nutmeg

1 teaspoon cracked black pepper

3-4 sprigs of fresh winter savory or lemon thyme

zest of 1 lemon

salt

100g (3½oz) Gruyère or Swiss cheese, grated

SAVOURY BREAD PUDDING

Preheat the oven to 220°C (425°F), Gas Mark 7. Cut the bread into 2.5cm (1 inch) cubes, arrange on a baking sheet and cook in the oven for 15 minutes until starting to crisp and turn golden. Remove from the oven and reduce the oven temperature to 200°C (400°F), Gas Mark 6.

Meanwhile, melt the butter in a frying pan over a medium heat and cook the leeks for 5–10 minutes until lightly golden. Add the wine or water and continue to cook until the leeks are tender.

Beat the eggs in a large bowl with the milk, then add the nutmeg, black pepper, herbs and lemon zest and season to taste with salt.

Sprinkle half the cheese in the bottom of a lightly greased casserole dish and add the bread, leeks and milk mixture. Cover with the remaining cheese, bringing some of the bread pieces to the surface. Cook in the preheated oven for 12–15 minutes until golden and just set. Serve hot.

Golden perfection

This dish can be made in hundreds of slightly different ways and is known by a selection of names including eggy bread, *pain perdu* and French toast, to name a few... The governing force is that it is rich, comforting and perfect for breakfast or dessert.

SERVES 4

4 large eggs

100g (3½oz) caster sugar

2-3 drops of vanilla extract

150ml (¼ pint) single cream or milk

4 thick slices of stale white bread, crusts removed

100g (3½oz) unsalted butter

Greek yoghurt, to serve

FOR THE POACHED PEARS

4 Conference pears, peeled and cut into quarters

200ml (7fl oz) red wine

50g (2oz) blackberries

50g (2oz) dried white mulberries (optional)

a pinch of ground ginger

1 teaspoon ground cinnamon

2 tablespoons sugar

DELUXE FRENCH TOAST

For the poached pears, place all the ingredients in a large pan, cover and bring to the boil. Reduce the heat and simmer gently for 15–20 minutes until the pears are tender. Carefully remove the fruit with a slotted spoon and set aside. Strain the liquid and return to the rinsed pan, then bubble over a high heat for a further 5–10 minutes until it thickens. Taste and add more sugar and cinnamon if necessary.

For the French toast, whisk the eggs until smooth, add the sugar, then continue whisking until the sugar starts to dissolve. Stir in the vanilla and cream or milk, then pour the mixture into a shallow dish. Cut the bread into triangles or fingers, if liked, and soak, a few pieces at a time, in the cream mixture for at least 1 minute on each side.

Melt the butter in a large frying pan over a medium heat and cook the bread in batches for 2–3 minutes, turning once, until lightly golden. Serve the hot French toast with the spiced fruit, a generous spoonful of Greek yoghurt and a drizzle of the cinnamon syrup.

METHOD #14

FLAVOURED BREADS

Dough has a taste all of its own. The balance of different grains and yeasty aroma provides a wealth of individual and distinctive-tasting breads. But for a radically unique bread, why not consider flavouring the dough with added ingredients? We will try almost anything once and sometimes the most unexpected experiments become a family favourite. The method varies, according to the texture you are trying to achieve, and even the colour you want.

FRUIT & VEGETABLES

Fruit can generally be incorporated raw and chopped, but if you want to add extra flavour cook it first, caramelizing it with some spices.

Vegetables can be more complicated as some are best braised or at least parboiled before being added to the dough. When you are preparing the flavouring ingredients, remember that they are going to be baked in the bread for extra time. If you want them to retain texture, reduce the pre-cooking time accordingly.

LIQUIDS

Infusing a bread with lots of potent aroma is easily done with a liquid. Instead of water, try using wine, cider, beer or even milk to make the dough. The quantities remain the same but the colour, taste and smell is very different. The other way to use a liquid flavouring is to soak another ingredient in it, such as raisins, then incorporate that ingredient into the dough once it has absorbed the flavour of the liquid. The Fig, Walnut & Red Wine Bread (see page 106) uses both of these techniques.

HERBS, NUTS & SPICES

Toast nuts and spices in a dry frying pan to heighten their aromas before adding them to your dough. Be bold and add enough to really permeate the dough with flavour. Getting the quantity right can be slightly tricky as the dough will increase in volume as it proves, so add a little more than you think you need to achieve a strongly scented or spiced loaf.

COLOURINGS

Children love eating colourful bread and it can be an exciting way to use unusual ingredients. Try using a few teaspoons of squid ink for a black bread or make a brightly coloured spiced bread by infusing the water with turmeric or saffron before adding it to the dough. These spices pack a big flavour punch, so balance carefully with some grated coconut, flaked almonds or other sweet ingredients.

HOW TO MAKE A FLAVOURED LOAF

1 Make sure the flavouring ingredients are at the same temperature as the dough, then add them to the dough.

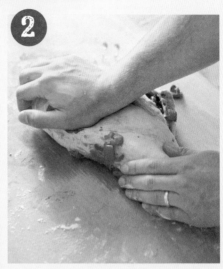

2 Mix the ingredients into the dough by kneading and folding for 2–3 minutes.

3 Leave to rise, knock back, shape and prove. Cook in a preheated oven at 220°C (425°F), Gas Mark 7, for 10 minutes, then 200°C (400°F), Gas Mark 6, for 30–40 minutes.

PUMPKIN BREAD

Makes 1 large loaf

500g (1lb) strong white flour, plus extra for dusting

10g (3/8 oz) fresh yeast

10g (3/8 oz) salt

350ml (12fl oz) tepid water

FOR THE FLAVOURINGS

150g (5oz) roasted diced pumpkin

2 tablespoons olive oil, plus extra for greasing

1 tablespoon maple syrup

1 teaspoon dried chilli flakes

Make a basic bread dough and knead it. Then follow the instructions above to finish the loaf.

Adding cooked vegetables to a plain dough can add instant flavour and texture. This recipe is special to us because it tastes both fresh and luxurious. Braising the fennel in butter before adding it to the dough softens it and the added flavour complements the creamy cheese as it melts over the earthy chestnuts.

MAKES 1 LARGE LOAF

50g (2oz) butter, plus extra for greasing

1 fennel bulb, cut into 3.5cm (1½ inch) dice

100ml (3½fl oz) white wine

salt and freshly ground black pepper

75g (3oz) blue cheese, crumbled

zest of 1 lemon

75g (3oz) cooked chestnuts, chopped

FOR THE DOUGH

500g (1lb) strong white flour, plus extra for dusting

20g (¾oz) fresh yeast

10g (⅜oz) salt

325ml (11fl oz) tepid water

FENNEL BREAD

Melt the butter in a heavy-based pan and cook the fennel over a medium heat for 5 minutes until golden. Add the white wine and simmer for 10–12 minutes until the fennel is tender. Drain and discard the liquid, then transfer the fennel to a bowl, season to taste and allow to cool. Stir in the blue cheese, lemon zest and chestnuts.

Make a basic bread dough and knead it following the instructions on pages 20–3. Spread the dough out flat, sprinkle the fennel mixture on top and knead into the dough until evenly distributed. Allow the dough to rise, knock back, shape and prove in the same way as a standard white tin loaf (see pages 24–31).

Preheat the oven to 220°C (425°F), Gas Mark 7, and cook the bread for 10 minutes, then reduce the temperature to 200°C (400°F), Gas Mark 6, and cook for a further 30–40 minutes. Turn out of the tin and allow to cool on a wire rack.

Any leftover bread can be stored in a plastic bag or wrapped in greaseproof paper where it will stay fresh for 2–3 days. Alternatively, store in the freezer for 2–3 months, having sliced the bread first so you can defrost only what you need.

Bread and wine is a classic partnership. In this recipe we have soaked the fruit and nuts in wine, infusing them with flavour, then used the wine to flavour the dough, giving it a rich umber colour and tannin depth.

MAKES 1 LARGE LOAF OR 2 SMALL LOAVES

250ml (8fl oz) red wine

200g (7oz) dried figs, roughly chopped

100g (3½oz) walnut pieces, roughly crushed

250g (8oz) strong white flour, plus extra for dusting

250g (8oz) strong wholemeal flour

20g (¾oz) fresh yeast

10g (⅜oz) salt

oil, for greasing

FIG, WALNUT & RED WINE BREAD

Place the wine, figs and walnuts in a pan and bring to the boil. Reduce the heat and simmer for 1–2 minutes, then transfer to a bowl, cover and leave to soak overnight, stirring occasionally.

Strain the figs and nuts and transfer the wine to a measuring jug. Top up with tepid water to make 300ml (½ pint). Make a basic bread dough using the wine mixture and the remaining ingredients and knead it following the instructions on pages 20–3. Spread the dough out flat, sprinkle the figs and nuts on top and knead into the dough until evenly distributed. Allow the dough to rise and knock back in the same way as a standard white loaf (see pages 24–5). Divide the dough in half and shape each piece into a tight roll, then leave to prove, covered, in greased loaf tins or on a greased baking sheet for 45 minutes.

Preheat the oven to 220°C (425°F), Gas Mark 7, and slash the tops of the loaves. Cook the bread in the oven for 10 minutes, then reduce the temperature to 200°C (400°F), Gas Mark 6, and cook for a further 30 minutes. Allow to cool on a wire rack.

Any leftover bread can be stored in a plastic bag or wrapped in greaseproof paper where it will stay fresh for 2–3 days. Alternatively, store in the freezer for 2–3 months, having sliced the bread first so you can defrost only what you need.

We were inspired to try our version of this unusual loaf by The Thoughtful Bread Company. The bread is designed to encourage children to eat more vegetables, due to its bright colour, but it is very tasty for grown-ups too.

SERVES 4

FOR THE BEETROOT BREAD

500g (1lb) strong white flour, plus extra for dusting

10g (⅜oz) fresh yeast

1 teaspoon salt

250ml (8fl oz) tepid water

150g (5oz) cooked beetroot, puréed

1 tablespoon olive oil, plus extra for greasing

FOR THE WALNUT & GOATS' CHEESE SALAD

150g (5oz) soft goats' cheese

32 wafer-thin slices of raw beetroot

150g (5oz) pickled walnuts

2 spring onions, sliced

1 pear, peeled, cored and finely diced

125g (4oz) raspberries

125g (4oz) baby beet leaves

3 tablespoons balsamic vinegar

2 tablespoons olive oil

1 tablespoon chopped chives

1 teaspoon caster sugar

zest of 1 lemon

salt and freshly ground black pepper

BEETROOT BREAD WITH WALNUT & GOATS' CHEESE SALAD

Make a basic bread dough with the flour, yeast, salt and water and knead it following the instructions on pages 20–3. Spread the dough out flat, arrange the puréed beetroot and oil on top and knead into the dough until evenly distributed. Allow the dough to rise, knock back, shape and prove in the same way as a standard white tin loaf (see pages 24–31).

Preheat the oven to 220°C (425°F), Gas Mark 7. Cook the bread in the oven for 30 minutes until the bottom sounds hollow when tapped. Allow to cool on a wire rack.

Once cooled, cut 4 slices of bread, spread a quarter of the goats' cheese on top of each slice and then cut in half diagonally. Arrange the beetroot slices, pickled walnuts, spring onions, pear, raspberries and salad leaves on 4 serving plates and top each salad with a slice of bread and goats' cheese.

Whisk together the remaining ingredients to make a dressing, season to taste and pour over the bread and salad. Serve immediately.

Potato bread has a consistency that is somewhat thicker than standard loaves and has much in common with gnocchi. Our version is a yeast-risen potato bread, and is extremely tasty served with devilled kidneys.

SERVES 4

500g (1lb) strong white flour,
plus extra for dusting

350g (11½oz) potatoes, peeled
and grated

250ml (8fl oz) tepid water

15g (½oz) fresh yeast, finely crumbled

50ml (2fl oz) olive oil, plus extra
for greasing

2 tablespoons chopped fresh dill

2 teaspoons salt

POTATO BREAD

Place all the ingredients into a large bowl, stir well with a wooden spoon, then turn out on to a floured work surface. Knead for 2–3 minutes, then return to the lightly oiled bowl, cover and leave to rise for 1–2 hours.

Knock back and shape the dough into a round loaf, then transfer to a floured peel or a lightly greased baking sheet or loaf tin. Cover again and leave to prove for 1 hour.

Preheat the oven to 200°C (400°F), Gas Mark 6. Slash a cross in the top of the dough, dust with extra flour, then cook in the oven for 45 minutes. Allow to cool on a wire rack.

Any leftover bread can be stored in a plastic bag or wrapped in greaseproof paper where it will stay fresh for 2–3 days. Alternatively, store in the freezer for 2–3 months, having sliced the bread first so you can defrost only what you need.

Metal saucepans make great alternatives to baking tins

If you want the bread on your table to be a talking point, this is the recipe for you! Bread has been baked in pots since ancient times, and today a standard terracotta flowerpot can make a beautiful loaf. You could add any flavouring ingredients that you fancy, but we've baked ours with flowers.

MAKES 4 LARGE OR 16 SMALL LOAVES

500g (1lb) strong white flour, plus extra for dusting

20g (¾oz) fresh yeast

50g (2oz) butter, softened

1 teaspoon salt

250ml (8fl oz) tepid water

1 tablespoon pot marigold (Calendula) petals

1 tablespoon rosemary or chive flowers

1 teaspoon dried rose petals

1-2 drops of orange blossom extract (optional)

FLOWERPOT BREAD

To make the dough, place the flour in a mixing bowl and crumble in the yeast. Rub the yeast into the flour with the fingertips until the mixture resembles fine breadcrumbs. Stir in the butter and salt, then start to work the dough, adding the water until it is pliable.

Knead the dough for 8–10 minutes until smooth and elastic.

Spread the dough out flat, sprinkle the flowers and orange blossom extract on top and knead into the dough until evenly distributed. Return to the bowl, cover and leave to rise in a warm place for 1–2 hours.

Line 3 large flowerpots (10cm/4 inches in diameter and 15cm/6 inches high) or 15 small flowerpots (5cm/ 2 inches in diameter and 7.5cm/3 inches high) with greaseproof paper. Knock back the dough, divide into portions and place the pieces in the pots. Cover and leave to prove for 1 hour.

Preheat the oven to 200°C (400°F), Gas Mark 6. Transfer the pots to a baking sheet and cook in the oven for 25–30 minutes until golden. Remove the bread from the pots and allow to cool on a wire rack. Discard the greaseproof paper and serve. If you like, you can return the bread to the pots to serve.

Any leftover bread can be stored in a plastic bag or wrapped in greaseproof paper where it will stay fresh for 2–3 days. Alternatively, pack in plastic bags and store in the freezer for 2–3 months.

The ideal bread for gardening fanatics

Our breakfast bap is perfect if you want a wholesome and hearty breakfast. Instead of just serving a plain roll with your breakfast, this recipe layers the dough with tasty ingredients and sets you up nicely for the day ahead.

MAKES 4 LARGE ROLLS

1 tablespoon olive oil, plus extra for greasing

1 red onion, finely diced

250g (8oz) strong white flour, plus extra for dusting

5g (¼oz) fresh yeast

5g (¼oz) salt

175ml (6fl oz) tepid water

25g (1oz) butter

100g (3½oz) mushrooms, sliced

1 teaspoon chopped fresh thyme

salt and freshly ground black pepper

6-12 cherry tomatoes, halved

BREAKFAST BAPS

Heat half the oil in a frying pan, add the onion and cook over a medium heat for 5–10 minutes until tender and lightly caramelized. Allow to cool.

Make a basic bread dough with the flour, yeast, salt and water and knead it following the instructions on pages 20–3. Spread the dough out flat, arrange the fried onion on top and knead into the dough until evenly distributed. Return to the bowl, cover and leave to rise for 1 hour.

Meanwhile, heat the butter in the frying pan and cook the mushrooms with the thyme until golden. Season to taste, transfer to a bowl and allow to cool. Heat the remaining oil in the frying pan, add the tomatoes and cook for 3–4 minutes until softened. Season and allow to cool.

Knock back the dough and roll out on a lightly floured work surface to 5mm (¼ inch) thick. Use a pastry cutter to cut out 16 rounds about 7cm (3 inches) in diameter. Arrange 4 of the rounds, well spaced, on a greased baking sheet. Brush with a little water and divide the mushrooms between them, leaving a border around the edges. Place a second round of dough on top of each and press lightly to stick it to the first. Arrange the onions on top, again leaving a border around the edges and brush with a little more water. Repeat with another round of dough and then the tomatoes. Top with the final dough rounds, press into place, cover and leave to prove for 45 minutes.

Preheat the oven to 230°C (450°F), Gas Mark 8. Remove the cover and mist the rolls with water, then cook in the oven for 12–15 minutes until lightly golden. Allow to cool on a wire rack.

Serve the rolls with a traditional fried breakfast.

METHOD #15

BAGUETTES

Making a baguette isn't difficult, but if you want to make a fantastic baguette then patience and practice are vital. The elements that make a good French stick are symmetrical shaping, exact proving times to create an array of random-sized aromatic holes in the dough, and precise scoring for a professional look. We tend to use a standard white dough for baguettes and make a few long ones from each batch to eat fresh; the rest we shape into mini sticks or the freezer.

MAKING

Make the dough, knead it and leave to rise following the instructions on pages 20–5. Turn out the dough on to a lightly floured surface, knock back (see page 25) and divide into 4 or 8 pieces. Arrange with the smoother sides facing down.

SHAPING

The most important stage of baguette making is the shaping so take your time and be gentle. Use your fingers to carefully flatten the dough into an oval shape with one of the pointed ends facing you.

Start by mentally dividing the dough into thirds from front to back. Fold the far third towards you over the middle third. Rotate the dough by 180° and repeat. Pat down each time to de-gas the dough. You now have a smart rectangle to work with.

Working along the far edge of the dough from right to left (if you are right-handed), use your left thumb to pin down the centre of the dough while your fingers pull the edge of the dough up and towards you. Then use the heel of your right hand to press the edge of the dough down. Slide along a bit and continue this motion to the end. Rotate the dough by 180° and repeat, this time folding the far edge all the way over so the seam is tucked underneath along the edge closest to you.

ROLLING

Roll the dough towards you so that the seam is right underneath. Then slightly overlap your flat hands over the middle of the dough and start rocking them with gentle downward pressure backwards and forwards. The way you move your hands will determine how uniform the shape becomes but try to relax and go with the flow. Gradually start to move your hands in arcs away from each other to extend the length of the baguette. Slowly move your hands apart as you make the arc shapes until you eventually reach the ends of the dough. The baguette should be wider in the centre and taper off at the ends. If you aren't completely satisfied with the shape of your baguette, return to the middle and repeat the process.

PROVING

Carefully transfer the shaped baguettes to a floured linen cloth, bringing a fold of fabric up between them to form a barrier and prevent them touching as they expand. Cover and leave to prove in a warm place for 1–2 hours.

COOKING

Transfer the baguettes to a lightly greased baking sheet and score a number of diagonal cuts at intervals down their length. Seven cuts is the traditional number for a French stick but each baker has their own style. Spray with water and cook in a preheated oven at 200°C (400°F), Gas Mark 6, for 10–15 minutes. Don't open the oven early or you'll stop that distinctive crust from forming.

FREEZING

If you want to bake some baguettes to serve on another day, reduce the baking time by 4–5 minutes and allow to cool. Wrap the baguettes individually in clingfilm and place in a plastic bag before freezing. Defrost thoroughly and cook in a preheated oven at 200°C (400°F), Gas Mark 6, for 5–8 minutes or until golden brown.

BAGUETTES

Makes 8 small sticks or 4 large baguettes

500g (1lb) strong white flour, plus extra for dusting

10g (³⁄₈oz) fresh yeast

10g (³⁄₈oz) salt

325ml (11fl oz) tepid water

To make this bread, follow the instructions opposite.

The ideal companion for some cheese and wine

METHOD #16

FOUGASSE

We love variety and that's why the fougasse has a special place in our oven. Essentially it is a basic flatbread, similar to focaccia. Its name comes from the Latin word for a hearth and this is because it was traditionally baked in the hot ashes of a bread oven as a kind of temperature gauge -- the time it took to bake would determine when the main bulk of bread could go in. The shape is supposed to resemble an ear of wheat, but be creative. We've taken to making our fougasse look like flames, curving the cuts to give them a more vibrant appearance.

MAKING

Make the dough, knead it and leave to rise for 1 hour, following the instructions on pages 20–5. Turn out the dough on to a lightly floured work surface, then divide it carefully into 6 elongated triangles or oval shapes and gently flatten them with your fingers without knocking all the air out.

SHAPING

The unique thing about fougasse is its decorative shape, but try not to over-complicate things. If you try to squeeze in too many little cuts, they are likely to close up again. We make a cut down the centre of the dough, without going to the edges, then make 2 more cuts fanning out each side. Try using a pizza wheel or a paring knife to make the cuts. Use your fingers to open up the slits, then place the shaped loaves on a floured peel or baking sheet ready for the oven. A generous dusting of cornflour will help them to come out of the oven looking even more golden and authentic.

COOKING

Bake fougasse in a preheated oven at 230°C (450°F), Gas Mark 8, for 15–20 minutes. As you are about to put your baking sheets into the oven or slide the loaves off the peel, spray the inside of the oven with a water mister. Do this again after you've put them in and close the door quickly. This gives them their distinctive crunchy crust and will help to keep the insides soft.

STORING

The design of this bread makes it perfect for hanging up in your kitchen. Reheat in the oven to freshen it up when you want to eat the bread. Alternatively, store in a bread bin to keep fresh for longer.

Fougasse can also be part-baked and frozen. Cook for three-quarters of the recommended time, then allow to cool on a wire rack, wrap tightly and store in the freezer. When you want to eat the bread, cook from frozen at 230°C (450°F), Gas Mark 8, for 12 minutes.

HOW TO SHAPE FOUGASSE

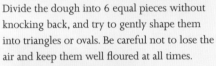

Divide the dough into 6 equal pieces without knocking back, and try to gently shape them into triangles or ovals. Be careful not to lose the air and keep them well floured at all times.

Make a small number of cuts through the dough to make a simple pattern, exercising some restraint. We cut 1 line down the centre and 2 cuts fanning out on each side.

FOUGASSE

Makes 6

500g (11b) strong white flour, plus extra for dusting

10g (⅜oz) fresh yeast

10g (⅜oz) salt

325ml (11fl oz) tepid water

cornflour, for dusting

To make this bread, follow the instructions above and opposite.

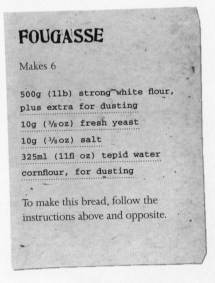

Use your fingers to tease the dough apart and transfer to a floured baking sheet or peel. Dust with cornflour. After cooking, allow to cool by hanging up in your kitchen from a hook.

If you are looking for a quintessentially English bread, look no further. We love to serve muffins for breakfast topped with smoked haddock and asparagus in a creamy sauce, but they are also delicious toasted and buttered for tea.

MAKES 10

500g (1lb) strong white flour, plus extra for dusting

10g (⅜oz) fresh yeast

10g (⅜oz) salt

325ml (11fl oz) tepid water

1 tablespoon sunflower oil

50g (2oz) semolina flour

ENGLISH MUFFINS

To make the dough, place the flour in a mixing bowl and crumble in the yeast. Rub the yeast into the flour with the fingertips until the mixture resembles fine breadcrumbs. Stir in the salt, then pour in the water and mix to a dough. Drizzle half the sunflower oil over the top, then turn out on to a lightly floured surface.

Knead the dough for 10 minutes until smooth and elastic, then return to the bowl, drizzle with the remaining oil, cover and leave to rise in a warm place for 1–2 hours.

When the dough has doubled in size, dust a work surface with semolina flour, turn out the dough and divide into 10 equal pieces. Flatten each with the heel of your hand or a rolling pin and shape into rounds 1–2.5cm (½–1 inch) thick. Dust with semolina flour and transfer to a floured baking sheet. Cover and leave to prove for 45 minutes. If you want to produce really uniform muffins, grease 10 stainless steel forming rings and allow the muffins to prove in them. Slide off the rings just before cooking.

Preheat a griddle or large, heavy-based frying pan and cook the muffins in batches. Cook for 1 minute, then turn over and cook the other side for 1 minute. If the muffins are browning too quickly, turn down the heat. Repeat for a total of 10 minutes, then remove from the pan and cool on a wire rack. If you want to freeze some, cook for just 5–6 minutes, cool and seal in freezer bags. Finish cooking from frozen for 8–10 minutes.

Use stainless steel rings for uniform muffins

For us, crumpets are Saturday afternoon comfort food. The bubbly surface is crying out for a thick layer of butter, which permeates into the spongy dough in golden rivulets, oozing out with every bite.

MAKES 10-12

500g (1lb) strong white flour

300ml (10fl oz) tepid milk

300ml (10fl oz) tepid water

5g (¼oz) fresh yeast

10g (⅜oz) salt

1 teaspoon baking powder

vegetable oil, for greasing

CRUMPETS

Mix the flour, milk and water in a mixing bowl using a whisk. Crumble in the yeast and whisk to form a smooth runny batter. Cover with clingfilm and leave in a warm place for 1–2 hours, or longer if you've got time, until the batter is bubbling. Whisk in the salt and baking powder.

Preheat a griddle until hot. Dip a piece of kitchen paper in vegetable oil and use to grease a stainless steel forming ring or crumpet ring, and the surface of the griddle. The griddle is hot enough for cooking if the oil does not smoke as you wipe it on.

To be safe, test one crumpet before you make the whole batch to check the batter is the right consistency. Place the crumpet ring on the griddle and spoon batter into the ring to the top. If the batter is too thin, it will leak out of the bottom of the ring – if so, whisk in a bit more flour. As the crumpet cooks, bubbles will rise to the surface. If the batter is too thick, no bubbles will appear – if so, whisk a little more water into the batter.

Cook the crumpet for 5 minutes, then turn over and cook the other side for 2–3 minutes. The base should be golden brown. If it is burnt, reduce the heat before you cook the others. Remove from the griddle and leave to cool on a wire rack or, if you are serving them immediately, wrap in a tea towel while you cook the rest.

To make pikelets, add 50g (2oz) more flour to the batter and cook by simply pouring spoonfuls of the batter straight on the hot griddle, without using crumpet rings. Be sure to grease the griddle, and cook the pikelets for 2–3 minutes on each side.

Ready to fill

BAGELS

Anyone who visits New York raves about the bagel shops there, telling mouth-watering stories of bagels layered with salt beef or salmon and cream cheese. Commercial bagel production has become big business, but to really enjoy the chewy texture and golden exterior you've got to make them yourself. The hole in the middle was designed for hanging the bagels on a piece of dowel or string, making for easy transport and display, but for the home baker it is the key to even cooking and an authentic appearance! Bagels are one of our favourite lunchtime snacks; we especially like the poaching process that adds extra flavour to a unique and delicious bread.

MAKING

Make a batch of dough by mixing the flour, yeast, salt, water, sugar and oil together and kneading for about 10 minutes until elastic. Return to the oiled bowl, cover with clingfilm and leave to rise in a warm place for 1 hour.

SHAPING

Knock back the dough, divide into 12 equal pieces and roll the pieces into sausage shapes. It helps to get an even thickness at this stage to make it easier to form the rings. If anything, make the ends slightly thicker than the middle. Wrap one of the sausages around the broadest part of your hand, overlapping the ends slightly in your palm. Roll your hands backwards and forwards on a lightly floured surface with some downward pressure to form a neat ring. When you become proficient with the technique, try rolling one in each hand at the same time. Don't worry if they look too thin as they will expand during proving.

PROVING

Place on a greased tray, cover with clingfilm brushed with oil and leave in a warm place to prove for 1 hour.

COOKING

Bagels are first poached in water flavoured with maple syrup, then baked in the oven. Choose a large pan, at least 10cm (4 inches) deep, for poaching the bagels. Fill with water and bring to the boil. Add the maple syrup to the water, then check the colour. The poaching liquid should be the colour of strong tea, so if it is too pale, add more syrup. Bagels puff up as they cook, so don't overcrowd the pan. As bagels float, they have to be turned halfway through cooking; the best tool for this is a slotted spoon.

After poaching, lift the bagels out of the pan and plunge into a bowl of iced water to stop them cooking and help create that chewy texture. Leave them to drain on a tea towel.

When all of your bagels have been poached, brush the top side with beaten egg, then coat with sesame seeds, poppy seeds or any other topping. Transfer the bagels to a greased baking sheet and cook in the oven until golden brown and glossy. See pages 126–127 for more details.

STORING

Any leftover bagels can be stored in a plastic bag or wrapped in greaseproof paper where they will stay fresh for 2–3 days. If you want to cook them in advance for eating on a later day, simply wrap individually in clingfilm after they have been poached and cooled, place in a plastic bag and freeze them. Defrost thoroughly and bake them as above when ready to eat.

NOW TRY: SALTY BAGELS

Sprinkle a generous amount of sea salt flakes over one side of the bagels after they've been poached.

NOW TRY: DILL BAGELS

Add 2 tablespoons of chopped fresh dill to the dough. Dill bagels are particularly good filled with cream cheese and smoked salmon.

NOW TRY: CHEESE & ONION BAGELS

Add 100g (3½oz) of grated cheese and 1 finely chopped onion to the dough. Fill the cooked bagels with honey-glazed ham and roasted red peppers.

HOW TO SHAPE & COOK BAGELS

Divide the dough into 12 and form each piece into a sausage, about 15cm (6 inches) long, by rolling your hands backwards and forwards while exerting gentle downward pressure.

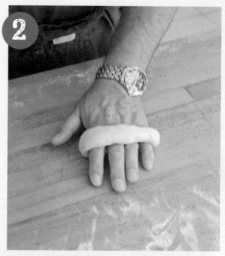

Flour your hands and wrap the dough around the broadest part of your hand, overlapping the ends under your palm. Roll backwards and forwards until you have an even ring.

Using a large slotted spoon, lift out the bagels and plunge them into a bowl of iced water for a few seconds. Then leave to drain on a tea towel.

Brush the bagels with beaten egg for extra golden shine. Sprinkle the sesame seeds on a plate and press the bagels into the seeds to coat.

Place the bagels on a greased tray and leave to prove, covered, in a warm place for 1 hour.

Bring a large pan of water and maple syrup to the boil. Place 3–4 bagels carefully into the liquid and poach for 2 minutes. Turn and poach for 2 minutes more.

Bake in a preheated oven at 200°C (400°F), Gas Mark 6, for 15 minutes until golden brown and glossy, then leave on a wire rack to cool.

SESAME BAGELS

Makes 12

500g (1lb) strong white flour, plus extra for dusting

5g (¼oz) fresh yeast, crumbled

10g (⅜oz) salt

250ml (8fl oz) tepid water

20g (¾oz) caster sugar

50ml (2fl oz) vegetable oil, plus extra for greasing

50ml (2fl oz) maple syrup

1 egg, beaten

2–4 tablespoons sesame seeds

Mix the flour, yeast, salt, water, sugar and oil to a dough and knead until elastic. Leave to rise for 1 hour, then follow the instructions above.

Dough balls are the perfect bite-sized snack. We like making them with a plain dough and serving with garlic butter, but dough balls are ideal for experimentation, so have fun and try adding chopped herbs, grated cheese, spices, cooked vegetables, pine nuts, pesto or harissa to the dough while mixing.

MAKES 30-40

500g (1lb) strong white flour, plus extra for dusting

20g (¾oz) fresh yeast

10g (⅜oz) salt

50ml (2fl oz) olive oil, plus extra for greasing and brushing

300ml (10fl oz) tepid water

FOR THE GARLIC BUTTER

150g (5 oz) butter

4 garlic cloves, crushed

DOUGH BALLS WITH GARLIC BUTTER

To make the dough, place the flour in a mixing bowl and crumble in the yeast. Rub the yeast into the flour with the fingertips until the mixture resembles fine breadcrumbs. Stir in the salt, then pour in the olive oil and water and mix to a dough.

Knead the dough for 5–10 minutes until smooth and elastic, then return to the bowl, cover and leave to rise in a warm place for 1 hour.

To make the garlic butter, heat 50g (2oz) of the butter in a small pan, add the garlic and simmer very gently for 2–3 minutes without browning. Allow to cool slightly, then transfer to a food processor, add the remaining butter and blend to combine. Transfer to ramekins and refrigerate for at least 1 hour before serving.

Preheat the oven to 220°C (425°F), Gas Mark 7, and grease 2 baking sheets. Transfer the dough to a lightly floured work surface, knock back and divide into balls about 25g (1oz) each, weighing the dough for accuracy if you like. Shape the balls by cupping in the palm of one hand and rolling on a floured surface or on your other hand. Transfer to the baking sheets and brush with a little olive oil.

Cook in the oven for 15 minutes until risen and firm. Brush the balls again with oil, then leave to cool on a wire rack or transfer immediately to a plate and serve hot with the garlic butter.

FOCACCIA

Most breads need butter, or even cheese or pâté, to make them into a satisfying snack, but focaccia is a meal in itself. It fills the plate without leaving you looking for the rest of the food to accompany it. That said, we do like to dip this bread in a good olive oil and some balsamic vinegar, but the point is it's delicious on its own. The dough can be adapted by adding air-dried ham, sun-dried tomatoes, olives, pesto or nuts, so once you've mastered the basics, have fun working the flavours.

MAKING

Make a basic olive oil dough using flour and semolina. Rub the yeast into the flour and semolina with your fingertips until the mixture resembles fine breadcrumbs, stir in the salt, then mix in the oil and tepid water. Use a dough scraper for mixing if you have one, and continue for 3–4 minutes until it starts to become elastic. Turn out the dough on to a lightly floured work surface and knead for 10 minutes. Now is the time to incorporate flavouring ingredients into the dough if you like. Return the dough to the bowl, cover with a damp cloth and leave to rise.

PROVING

Turn the dough out into a greased roasting tin or baking tray and gently spread into the corners with your fingertips. Try not to stretch the dough, just spread it out. Cover and leave to prove. Knock back the dough with your fingertips to form a surface of dimples. Cover again and leave for a final prove.

ADDING TOPPINGS

Now add the topping of your choice. Stick herbs into the dimples or sprinkle coarse salt, seeds or spices over the top and drizzle with oil.

COOKING

Cook in the oven until lightly golden brown, then transfer to a wire rack and brush with oil before serving. Focaccia is best enjoyed fresh but can be frozen in a sealed plastic bag.

ROSEMARY & SEA SALT FOCACCIA

Makes 1 large loaf

500g (1lb) strong white flour, plus extra for dusting

20g (¾oz) semolina

15g (½oz) fresh yeast

10g (⅜oz) salt

50ml (2fl oz) olive oil, plus extra for greasing

325ml (11fl oz) tepid water

FOR THE TOPPING

3–4 rosemary stems, divided into individual sprigs

1 teaspoon coarse sea salt

4 tablespoons olive oil

To make this bread, follow the instructions above and opposite.

HOW TO MAKE FOCACCIA

Mix all the ingredients to make a dough and knead for 10 minutes until smooth and elastic. Return to the bowl, cover and leave to rise in a warm place for 1–2 hours.

Turn out the dough into a greased roasting tin and knock it back gently so that it fills the tin. Cover with clingfilm brushed with oil and leave to prove for 45 minutes.

Knock back again with your fingers and leave to prove again for 30 minutes. Stick small rosemary sprigs into the dough, sprinkle with the sea salt and drizzle with half the oil.

Cook in a preheated oven at 200°C (400°F), Gas Mark 6, for 25 minutes. Brush with the remaining olive oil while the bread is cooling on a wire rack.

Olive oil breads like focaccia are perfect for use as breadcrumbs in pasta dishes. This meal is an excellent way to use up day-old bread in a creative way. Bottarga is an unusual ingredient that goes extremely well with the breadcrumbs. This salted and air-dried mullet roe adds a distinctive taste, but if you don't have any, then extra baked breadcrumbs will fill the gap.

SERVES 4–6

75g (3oz) day-old focaccia breadcrumbs

25g (1oz) bottarga, grated

2 tablespoons olive oil

50g (2oz) butter

1 shallot, finely diced

2–4 garlic cloves, finely chopped

1 teaspoon chopped fresh oregano

300g (10oz) clams in shells, fresh or from a jar

50g (2oz) chorizo, finely diced (optional)

100ml (3½fl oz) white wine

1 tablespoon crème fraîche

salt and freshly ground black pepper

75g (3oz) linguine per person, cooked, to serve

CLAM LINGUINE WITH BREADCRUMBS & BOTTARGA

Preheat the oven to 180°C (350°F), Gas Mark 4. Place the breadcrumbs on a baking sheet with the bottarga, drizzle with half the olive oil and cook in the preheated oven for 10 minutes until golden.

Clean the fresh clams, discarding any that are open or don't shut when you tap them.

Heat the butter in a large, wide pan, add the shallot and garlic and cook gently for 5 minutes until softened. Add the oregano, clams and chorizo, if using, and cook for about 3 minutes to brown the chorizo.

Add the wine and simmer for 4–5 minutes until reduced a little and all the clams have opened. Discard any that remain shut. Stir in half the breadcrumb mixture and the crème fraîche. Season to taste, toss with the cooked pasta and the remaining olive oil and divide between the serving plates. Sprinkle with the remaining breadcrumbs and serve immediately.

Baked breadcrumbs are the poor man's Parmesan

We've been making and eating pizza for years and it is has lost none of its appeal. It's one of the few things we completely agree on — that a homemade dough is always cheaper, healthier and tastier than its takeaway counterpart.

MAKES 3-4

FOR THE PIZZA DOUGH

500g (1lb) strong white flour, plus extra for dusting

15g (½oz) fresh yeast

10g (⅜oz) salt

325ml (11fl oz) tepid water

50ml (2fl oz) olive oil

FOR THE TOPPING

6 tablespoons olive oil

4-6 garlic cloves, finely chopped

zest of 1 lemon

3-4 rosemary stems, divided into sprigs

salt and freshly ground black pepper

12 new potatoes, very thinly sliced

150g (5oz) mozzarella, torn into chunks

3-4 tablespoons capers (optional)

POTATO & ROSEMARY PIZZAS

To make the dough, place the flour in a mixing bowl and crumble in the yeast. Rub the yeast into the flour with the fingertips until the mixture resembles fine breadcrumbs. Stir in the salt, then pour in the water and olive oil and mix to a dough.

Knead the dough for 8–10 minutes until smooth and elastic, then return to the bowl, cover and leave to rise in a warm place for 1–2 hours. Turn out the dough, knock back and divide into 3 or 4 balls. Leave the balls of dough to rest on a floured surface for 10–15 minutes.

To make a flavoured oil for the topping, heat the olive oil in a small pan, add the garlic and cook gently for 2–3 minutes without browning. Add the lemon zest and half the rosemary and season to taste. Allow to cool.

To shape the dough, push down in the centre of one of the balls with the heel of your hand and stretch the dough away from you. Rotate the flattened dough on an evenly floured work surface until you form a fairly regular round shape, at least 20cm (8 inches) in diameter. Be sure to push from the centre outwards so that the edges are thicker than the middle to stop the topping dripping off the edges. Carefully lift the pizza base on to a floured baking sheet or peel and repeat with the other balls of dough.

Preheat the oven to 240°C (475°F), Gas Mark 9. Brush the flavoured oil generously over the pizza bases and top with the potato slices. Scatter over the mozzarella, remaining rosemary and capers, if using. Drizzle with a little more flavoured oil and season well. Cook in the oven, on the baking sheets or preheated baking stones, for 10 minutes or until the dough is cooked through. Serve immediately.

In many cuisines around the world there are recipes for dough being folded in half and stuffed with a filling. This Italian-inspired recipe is currently our favourite combination and can be baked or fried.

MAKES 4

4 Toulouse or other spicy sausages

1 tablespoon olive oil

100ml (3½fl oz) red wine

12-16 cherry tomatoes, halved

1 green pepper, cored, deseeded and diced

150g (5oz) canned butter beans, rinsed and drained

150g (5oz) mozzarella, torn into chunks

50g (2oz) pitted olives

salt and freshly ground black pepper

1 quantity of pizza dough (see page 134)

basil leaves, to garnish

FOR THE SAUCE

2 tablespoons olive oil

1 onion, diced

2 garlic cloves, chopped

400g (13oz) can chopped tomatoes

6-12 basil leaves

25g (1oz) capers

1 tablespoon balsamic vinegar

1 teaspoon chopped fresh oregano

1 teaspoon sugar

1 bay leaf

SPICY SAUSAGE CALZONE

Cut the sausages into 5–6 pieces each. Heat the olive oil in a frying pan, add the sausage pieces and cook for 10–15 minutes until cooked through and golden. Add the wine and simmer for 10 minutes until the liquid has reduced to a few tablespoons. Transfer to a bowl and leave to cool, then add the tomatoes, green pepper, butter beans, mozzarella and olives. Season to taste and stir to combine.

To make the sauce, heat the olive oil in a heavy-based pan, add the onion and garlic and cook for 5–10 minutes until softened. Add the remaining ingredients and simmer for 15–20 minutes until thickened. Season to taste, remove the bay leaf and blend the sauce with a hand-held electric blender or food processor until smooth.

Preheat the oven to 240°C (475°F), Gas Mark 9. Allow the dough to rise, then shape it into 4 x 20cm (8 inch) rounds, following the instructions on page 134. Place one-quarter of the filling mixture on each of the pizza bases, arranging it to one side and leaving a 2.5cm (1 inch) border around the edge. Brush the border with water, then fold the empty side of the dough over the top of the filling and pinch the edges together to seal the parcels. Transfer to floured baking sheets or peels. Cook in the oven for 10–15 minutes or until the dough is cooked through. Reheat the tomato sauce and drizzle over the calzones, garnish with some basil and serve.

METHOD #19

BRIOCHE

Brioche defies convention by coming out of the oven light and ethereal despite containing a surprising amount of heavy butter. The consistency is utterly unique: a bit like a cake with a soft and buttery crust but the yeasty undertones of a good loaf. This duality is what makes it equally suited to spreading with a sweet apricot jam or a wedge of chicken liver parfait. You might assume brioche is difficult to make but the truth is that it is fairly easy.

PREPARING

Place all the ingredients, including the milk, in the refrigerator for a couple of hours before you start so the dough does not become oily as you work it. Before you add the butter, try to soften it by beating it with a rolling pin rather than allowing it to warm up. Cut the softened butter into cubes with a butter knife before incorporating it into the dough.

MAKING

Knead the dough for 10 minutes both before and after adding the butter. If you use a food mixer with a dough hook, you will obviously shorten the time considerably. To decide whether the dough has been kneaded enough, try the window test (see page 23). Shape the dough into a ball, return to the mixing bowl, cover and leave in the refrigerator overnight. This will allow the soft dough to firm up so it will be easier to shape the following day.

PROVING

Divide the dough into rolls or loaves, transfer to a greased baking sheet or floured peel, cover and leave to prove for 3–4 hours. The extra time needed is for the yeast to warm up after being chilled overnight.

COOKING

Glaze the brioche with beaten egg and cook until the buttery crust turns golden. Any leftover brioche can be stored in a bread bin where it will stay fresh for 3–4 days. It is surprisingly good toasted. Alternatively, store in the freezer for 2–3 months.

NOW TRY: BAKED BRIOCHE & CAMEMBERT PARCEL

Roll the chilled dough into a square about 5mm (¼ inch) thick. Place a 250g (8oz) piece of Camembert on the dough and fold up like a parcel, enclosing the cheese. Turn over, seam side down, on to a greased baking sheet and brush with beaten egg, then chill for 1 hour. You could make some holes through the dough and insert thin slices of garlic or sprigs of thyme to flavour the cheese as it melts. Score the top with a sharp knife for decoration and cook in a preheated oven at 200°C (400°F), Gas Mark 6, for 15 minutes.

BRIOCHE

Makes 2 small loaves

400g (13oz) strong white flour, plus extra for dusting

10g (⅜oz) fresh yeast, crumbled

1 teaspoon salt

75ml (3fl oz) milk

40g (1½oz) caster sugar

4 eggs, beaten, plus extra to glaze

150g (5oz) butter, softened and diced, plus extra for greasing

To make brioche, follow the instructions below and opposite.

HOW TO MAKE BRIOCHE

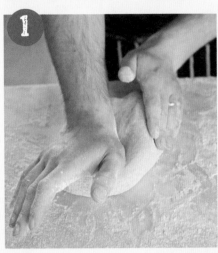

Mix the chilled flour, yeast, salt, milk, sugar and eggs to form a dough. Knead for 8–10 minutes on a floured surface.

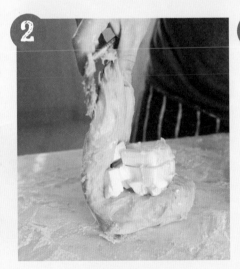

Add the butter and knead for 10 minutes. Chill overnight. Shape the dough into loaves, cover and leave to prove for 3–4 hours.

Brush the loaves all over with beaten egg, to glaze. Cook the brioche in a preheated oven at 220°C (425°F), Gas Mark 7, for 10 minutes then reduce the temperature to 200°C (400°F), Gas Mark 6, for a further 15–20 minutes.

We first discovered this style of baking by mistake when we proved a batch of Cinnamon Twirls too closely together in a tin and ended up with one large Cinnamon Twirl. It was so good that we decided to try it again with brioche! This is known as Brioche Nanterre, where the small balls of dough fuse together during the proving process. The great thing about this style of loaf is that it is perfect for tearing apart and sharing.

MAKES 2 LOAVES

1 quantity of Brioche dough
(see page 139)

100g (3½oz) soft dried apricots,
finely chopped

3 rosemary stems, divided into
individual sprigs

APRICOT & ROSEMARY BRIOCHE

Make the brioche dough and chill overnight, following the instructions on page 138–9.

Divide the dough into 30 pieces and shape each into a ball. Take the balls in your palm, one at a time, and use the thumb of your other hand to squeeze a teaspoon of chopped apricots and a small sprig of rosemary into each ball. Shape again into tight balls to enclose the filling. Arrange 15 brioche balls in each of 2 greased loaf tins, cover and leave to prove for 2 hours.

Preheat the oven to 200°C (400°F), Gas Mark 6. Glaze the brioche by brushing the surface with beaten egg, then cook in the oven for 20 minutes until golden. Allow to cool on a wire rack.

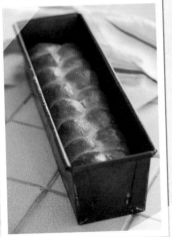

Fresh from the oven

We usually prefer savoury snacks but every so often we like to indulge in a sweet bread, like these twirls, to boost our sugar levels. You can adjust the filling with your own variations: we like adding some chopped baked apple and stewed blackberries, or raisins and chopped nuts for a festive treat.

MAKES 12

250g (8oz) strong white flour, plus extra for dusting

5g (¼oz) fresh yeast

75ml (3fl oz) tepid water

50g (2oz) caster sugar

3 teaspoons ground cinnamon

a pinch of salt

50g (2oz) butter, melted, plus extra for greasing

1 egg, beaten, plus extra to glaze

icing sugar, for dusting

CINNAMON TWIRLS

To make the dough, place the flour in a mixing bowl and crumble in the yeast. Rub the yeast into the flour with the fingertips until the mixture resembles fine breadcrumbs. Stir in the water and mix until smooth. Add half the sugar, 1 teaspoon of the cinnamon and the salt. Knead well, cover and leave in a warm place to rise.

Once the dough has risen, knock it back and make a small well in the middle. Place the melted butter and egg in the well and mix to combine. The dough will be very sticky so use a dough scraper to fold from the edge into the centre, rotating the bowl as you go. Once combined, cover and leave to rise again. Repeat this folding process every 10–15 minutes for 1 hour, then leave the dough to rise for a final hour until doubled in size.

Turn out the dough on to a floured surface and flatten using your fingertips into a rectangle 25 x 30cm (10 x 12 inches). Brush with beaten egg and sprinkle with another 1 teaspoon of the cinnamon and the remaining caster sugar. Roll up the dough tightly from one of the short sides and cut into 12 equal slices.

Transfer the twirls to greased baking sheets, cover and leave to prove for 45 minutes or until doubled in size. Preheat the oven to 200°C (400°F), Gas Mark 6, and place a roasting tin in the bottom.

Cook the twirls in the oven for 20 minutes until golden, pouring a cupful of hot water into the roasting tin as you put them in the oven. Cool on a wire rack. Dust with icing sugar and the remaining cinnamon before serving.

you cut, I'll choose

METHOD #20

DOUGHNUTS

At first glance, doughnuts may not seem to fit into the bread category, but they are made by mixing a yeasty dough with a rich batter. If you want to really enjoy these doughnuts, eat them while they are still warm, covered in granulated sugar. You can shape the dough into balls, or go for the iconic ring doughnuts, for which you will need pastry cutters or a special doughnut cutter for shaping.

PREPARING

The further in advance that you can start making doughnuts, the better. Like brioche, the dough is soft and any extra time in the refrigerator will help with the shaping process. Make sure you have fresh oil for frying so that they don't absorb any other flavours as they cook.

DOUGHNUTS

Makes 15–20

15g (½oz) fresh yeast
....
250ml (8fl oz) tepid water
....
500g (1lb) plain flour, plus extra for dusting
....
140g (4½oz) unsalted butter
....
200g (7oz) caster sugar
....
3 eggs
....
1 teaspoon salt
....
2 teaspoons vanilla extract
....
vegetable oil, for frying
....
granulated sugar, for dusting
....

To make doughnuts, follow the instructions opposite.

MAKING

Crumble the yeast into a bowl, add the water and whisk until dissolved. Add 100g (3½oz) of the flour, stir well and leave in a warm place for 1 hour until bubbly. Beat the butter in a large mixing bowl until softened, then add the sugar and continue beating until light and fluffy. Add the eggs, one at a time, and continue beating until fully incorporated then add the salt and vanilla extract.

Mix the remaining flour and the yeast mixture into the bowl with a wooden spoon or dough hook to form a soft dough. Cover and leave to rise in a warm place for 1–2 hours. Knock back the dough, cover again and chill in the refrigerator for 3–4 hours.

SHAPING

Divide the dough into 2 batches and keep one batch in the refrigerator while you work with the other. Turn out one batch on to a floured surface and shape by hand into balls

2.5–5cm (1–2 inches) across. Alternatively, to make ring doughnuts, roll out the dough to 1cm (½ inch) thick and cut out rings with a well-floured doughnut cutter or 2 pastry cutters of different sizes, ensuring the hole in the middle is at least 5cm (2 inches) across. Transfer the doughnuts to a tray covered with greaseproof paper and leave uncovered for 10–15 minutes.

COOKING

Heat the vegetable oil in a large pan or deep-fat fryer to 180°C (350°F). Fry just 2 or 3 doughnuts at a time to keep the oil temperature constant. Dip a metal spatula into the hot oil, then use it to lift up a doughnut from the tray. Lower the doughnut into the oil and cook until it is golden underneath, then turn it over and cook until the other side is golden. Drain the cooked doughnuts on a triple layer of kitchen paper and pat off any excess oil.

Place some granulated sugar into a paper bag and shake the doughnuts in the bag to coat in the sugar.

NOW TRY: CINNAMON DOUGHNUTS

Add a teaspoon of cinnamon to the granulated sugar in the paper bag and mix together before you coat the doughnuts with sugar.

NOW TRY: JELLY DOUGHNUTS

Roll out the doughnut dough to about 6mm (5/16 inch) thick and cut out rounds about 7cm (3 inches) across. Place a teaspoonful of strawberry jam or jelly in the middle of half the rounds, then brush round the edges with beaten egg. Top each with a second round, then pinch the edges together to seal. Re-form into a small ball and allow to rise as normal before frying.

you can inject plain doughnuts with jelly, too

This recipe takes a basic doughnut and gives it an exotic twist. These dumplings are much quicker to make than standard doughnuts because the dough doesn't need to firm up in the refrigerator. Instead, we spoon the soft batter straight into hot oil and serve immediately. If you want to please a crowd of hungry people at a party, this dish is a winner.

MAKES 12-15

250g (8oz) plain flour

5g (¼oz) fresh yeast

150ml (¼pint) tepid water

50g (2oz) caster sugar

50g (2oz) unsalted butter, softened

1 egg

2 bananas, mashed

a pinch of salt

vegetable oil, for frying

vanilla ice cream, to serve

FOR THE CARAMEL SAUCE

125g (4oz) brown sugar

40ml (1½fl oz) double cream

25g (1oz) butter

BANANA DUMPLINGS

Place the flour in a mixing bowl and crumble in the yeast. Rub the yeast into the flour with the fingertips until the mixture resembles fine breadcrumbs. Pour in the water and mix to a soft dough. Cover and leave to rest in a warm place for 1 hour.

To make the sauce, place all the ingredients in a heavy-based pan and bring to the boil. Reduce the heat and simmer for 4–5 minutes until the sauce thickens.

Place the sugar, butter and egg in another bowl and beat until smooth. Gradually incorporate the dough, then add the mashed bananas and salt. Heat the vegetable oil in a large pan or deep-fat fryer to 180°C (350°F). Use 2 dessertspoons to shape the dough into rough lozenges about 5cm (2 inches) across and drop them into the hot oil, a few at a time. Cook for a few minutes on each side until golden. Serve the hot dumplings drizzled with the sauce.

Every year it has become a family tradition at our house to eat this dense, sweet fruit bread as a festive treat. Stollen can be stored frozen for up to 2 months, so bake it in advance if you like to get ahead with your Christmas preparations.

MAKES 2 LOAVES

200g (7oz) marzipan, diced

100g (3½oz) raisins

100g (3½oz) mixed candied peel, chopped

50g (2oz) flaked almonds

50g (2oz) glacé cherries

50ml (2fl oz) Jamaican rum or orange juice

½ teaspoon ground cardamom

1 tablespoon lemon zest

a pinch of ground cinnamon

50g (2oz) butter, melted

icing sugar, for dusting

FOR THE DOUGH

500g (1lb) plain flour

40g (1½oz) fresh yeast

5g (¼oz) salt

225ml (7½fl oz) tepid milk

100g (3½oz) butter, melted and cooled, plus extra for greasing

40g (1½oz) caster sugar

1 large egg, beaten

STOLLEN

To make the dough, sift the flour into a mixing bowl and crumble in the yeast. Rub the yeast into the flour with the fingertips until the mixture resembles fine breadcrumbs, then stir in the salt, milk, butter, sugar and beaten egg and mix to a dough. Work the dough until it starts to become silky and smooth like a standard bread dough. Knead the dough for 10 minutes until smooth and elastic, then return to the bowl, cover and leave to rise in a warm place for 1–2 hours.

To make the filling, mix the marzipan, raisins, peel, almonds, cherries, rum or orange juice, cardamom, lemon zest and cinnamon in a mixing bowl and set aside.

Divide the dough into 2 pieces and gently knock out the air. Shape into 2 rectangles, about 30 x 15cm (12 x 6 inches). Spread the filling on top of the dough and roll up, tucking the ends underneath, to form 2 thick sausage shapes. Transfer to a lightly greased baking sheet, cover with a tea towel and leave to prove in a warm place for 2–4 hours.

Preheat the oven to 180°C (350°F), Gas Mark 4. Cook the stollen in the oven for 40 minutes until golden. Transfer to a wire rack and brush with the melted butter. Dust generously with icing sugar and allow to cool.

Wrap the stollen in greaseproof paper and store in a sealed cake tin or bread bin, where it will stay fresh for 1 week.

These traditional breads are well worth baking at least once. The golden orange colour of the dough is part of the allure, but the faint spice also makes them extremely tasty. You can either form them into standard round rolls or, if you want to try another variation, shape them into curly S-shapes. We make the dough with half lard and half butter, but you could use all butter if you prefer. Serve with a cup of tea and some clotted cream.

MAKES 12

a pinch of saffron threads

50ml (2fl oz) tepid water

500g (1lb) strong white flour, plus extra for dusting

60g (2½oz) butter, diced, plus extra for greasing and brushing

60g (2½oz) lard, diced

½ teaspoon salt

10g (⅜oz) fresh yeast, crumbled

75g (3oz) caster sugar

1 large egg, beaten

100ml (3½fl oz) tepid milk

100g (3½oz) currants or raisins

clotted cream, to serve

SAFFRON BUNS

Preheat the oven to 180°C (350°F), Gas Mark 4. Place the saffron threads in an ovenproof dish and place in the preheated oven for 2–3 minutes to dry out. Transfer to a mortar and grind to a powder with a pestle. Place in a small bowl with the water and leave to infuse for 10–15 minutes.

Meanwhile, place the flour in a mixing bowl with the butter, lard and salt. Rub the fat into the flour with the fingertips until the mixture resembles fine breadcrumbs. Stir in the yeast and sugar, then add the beaten egg, milk and saffron water. Gradually mix the ingredients to a dough and turn on to a floured surface. Knead the dough for 8–10 minutes until smooth and elastic, adding the currants near the end of the kneading time.

Divide the dough into 12 equal pieces and shape into rolls. Alternatively, roll into 12cm (5 inch) sausages, then curl the ends in opposite directions and tuck underneath. Transfer to greased baking sheets, cover and leave to prove in a warm place for 1–2 hours or until doubled in size.

Preheat the oven to 220°C (425°F), Gas Mark 7. Cook the buns in the oven for 12–15 minutes until golden. Transfer to a wire rack and brush with extra butter, then allow to cool. Serve with clotted cream.

Have fun and play with the shape

5

QUICK BREADS

INTRODUCTION TO
QUICK BREADS

The resurgence in home baking sadly doesn't fit well with everyone's lifestyle. Taking the time to slow down and bake is impossible for some people. This chapter is for all of you who struggle to find enough hours in the day. Instead of waiting for yeast to get the dough to rise, this selection of quick breads uses other raising agents to increase the volume of the dough using a simple chemical reaction. The best thing about quick breads is that it is easy to keep the ingredients ready to hand -- with a quick raid of a well-stocked storecupboard you can be baking in minutes.

THE LAZY LOAF

Baking bread is hard work and takes time to fit into your daily routine. Quick breads reduce the time that you have to set aside but still offer tasty homemade food. When you are short of time or have guests arriving imminently, you'll find that a loaf of soda bread or a batch of muffins is quick to make and throw into the oven.

If you need to be persuaded to try some of the recipes in this section, imagine taking away all of the rules, constraints and discipline associated with traditional baking and replacing them with a loaf made in a fraction of the time. The simplest quick breads are made by mixing together the dry ingredients with the wet ingredients and baking immediately.

THE MAGIC INGREDIENT

Baking powder (a combination of bicarbonate of soda and cream of tartar) is the raising agent used in most quick breads. The acidic cream of tartar and alkaline bicarbonate of soda react when they come into contact with water. This is why, once you have added the

liquid to your dough, it is sensible to bake it quickly and not waste all of the expanding carbon dioxide bubbles that will give it a light texture. It also explains why most commercial baking powders have a little flour or other starch added to them, to absorb any moisture that may get in during storage. After all, no one wants an exploding tub of baking powder in their cupboard.

Some recipes don't call for cream of tartar as they use an acidic liquid like buttermilk to start the reaction with the bicarbonate of soda instead.

DIY BAKING POWDER

Although baking powder is readily available, it is very easy to make your own at home. All you will need are two key ingredients: cream of tartar and bicarbonate of soda.

Combine ½ teaspoon of cream of tartar with ¼ teaspoon of bicarbonate of soda to make the equivalent of 1 teaspoon of baking powder. We scale this up and spoon 1 tablespoon of bicarbonate of soda and 2 tablespoons of cream of tartar into a small

waiting for your bread to cool is a test of patience

The more, the merrier — variety is the spice of life

sealable jar and shake together. We use the mixture within 1 month, using ¾ teaspoon of our DIY baking powder when a recipe calls for 1 teaspoon of baking powder.

OTHER INGREDIENTS

Quick breads offer a lot of flexibility to explore different types of flours and add different textures to the dough. We love to try out different flours in these breads, and also add a selection of other ingredients, such as wheatgerm, rolled oats or linseeds to increase the fibre. The evolution of soda bread (see page 158) to wheaten (see page 160) is just this and you can try a similar approach with all the recipes in this section. The similarity in texture to cakes makes some quick breads, such as banana bread (see page 166), perfect for sweetening up and experimenting with inventive flavours. Once you have understood the basic ratios of ingredients, you can experiment with all sorts of flavours to create your own unique sweet breads.

USING UP DAY-OLD BREAD

Quick breads have a crumb texture that lends itself to toasting and this is the best way to enjoy a loaf like soda bread on the second day. That said, we have grown up with a slightly less healthy but extremely tasty tradition. Fried sliced soda bread or wheaten is delicious. Fried farls, made from soda bread dough, are a key part of a breakfast fry-up. Along with fried meats and pancakes, they will give you enough energy to work all day long – or sit down and have a wee nap.

BATTERS & DOUGHS

Quick bread doughs tend to have a much wetter consistency than standard bread doughs and this makes it easy to pour out the dough into a mould like a batter. For the likes of cornbread you can actually use a ladle or spoon to drop the bread on to a hot skillet. Some, like soda bread, are slightly firmer due to a higher flour to liquid ratio, but the dough should still be pourable.

Essentially, if your dough is too thick to pour then it is probably not wet enough. Remember that the raising agents need liquid to activate them, and you could end up with a very unappetizing bread.

PERFECTING YOUR TECHNIQUE

The techniques used to make quick breads differ from those used to make yeast-risen breads, so here are some hints and tips.

CREAMING

This is a technique often used in cake baking and combines the sugar and butter by beating together into a smooth and fluffy cream. Use a wooden spoon to beat the mixture until it is pale and light. This captures air bubbles, which react when you gently fold in the rest of the ingredients.

FOLDING IN

We use a metal spoon to fold the remaining ingredients into the creamed mixture. A metal spoon has a sharper edge than a wooden spoon and prevents the air bubbles being squashed out of the mixture. It's a little extra washing up but definitely worth the effort.

RUBBING IN

We mix butter into flour by rubbing in with our fingertips or blending in a food processor until the mixture resembles fine breadcrumbs. This process adds air and gives the dough a flaky texture. When the fat melts during baking it contributes to the layers – perfect for scones!

Soda bread is a family tradition that has served us well. This is the perfect bread to mix together when you're in a rush and want something freshly baked to go with a quick lunchtime soup. It can be cooked as traditional loaves, or shaped into individual farls. Enjoy spread with butter, or fry in bacon fat as a tasty addition to a fry-up.

MAKES 2 LOAVES

500g (1lb) plain flour, plus extra for dusting

4 teaspoons baking powder

10g (⅜oz) salt

300ml (½ pint) buttermilk

butter, for greasing

SODA BREAD

Preheat the oven to 200°C (400°F), Gas Mark 6, and grease a large baking sheet. Mix all the dry ingredients together in a large mixing bowl and make a well in the middle. Gradually add enough buttermilk to make a soft but not wet dough. Knead the dough on a floured work surface for 2–3 minutes, then divide the dough into 2 pieces and shape each into a round about 5cm (2 inches) thick. Transfer to the prepared baking sheet, dust with flour and cut a deep cross in the top. Cook in the oven for 20–25 minutes until well risen, golden and it sounds hollow when tapped on the base. Transfer to a wire rack to cool.

To make farls, shape each piece of dough into a flat circle 1–2cm (½–1 inch) thick. Score the dough into 4 wedges, cutting about one-third of the way through. Cook on a preheated hot griddle, dusted with flour, for 4–5 minutes on each side until golden and cooked through.

Any leftover soda bread can be wrapped in greaseproof paper or clingfilm where it will stay fresh for 2–3 days. After this, it can be toasted or fried in oil. Consume within 1 week.

Cut one-third of the way through

Wheaten bread is so simple to make that it is a very useful recipe to have in reserve. The addition of oatmeal and/or wheatgerm adds more texture to the bread; feel free to experiment by adding some seeds or nuts as well, giving them a rough bashing with a rolling pin if they are too large. Like soda bread, wheaten can also be cooked on a floured griddle to make farls (see page 158).

SERVES 4

450g (14½oz) strong wholemeal flour, plus extra for dusting

2 tablespoons wheatgerm (optional)

2 tablespoons oatmeal (optional)

1 teaspoon cream of tartar

1 teaspoon bicarbonate of soda

2 teaspoons caster sugar

½ teaspoon salt

350ml (12fl oz) buttermilk

oil, for greasing

TO SERVE

12 dry-cured streaky bacon rashers

4 oysters, shucked

butter, for spreading

WHEATEN DREDGERMAN'S BREAKFAST

Preheat the oven to 200°C (400°F), Gas Mark 6, and grease a baking sheet. Mix all the dry ingredients together in a large mixing bowl and make a well in the middle. Gradually add enough buttermilk to make a soft but not wet dough. Knead the dough on a floured work surface for 2–3 minutes, then shape into a round about 25cm (10 inches) across. Transfer to the prepared baking sheet and cut a deep cross in the top. Cook in the oven for about 45 minutes until well risen, golden and it sounds hollow when tapped on the base. Transfer to a wire rack to cool a little.

Place the bacon in a cold frying pan, turn on the heat and allow the heat to increase until the fat comes out of the bacon. Cook until crisp, turning once. When the bacon is cooked, add the oysters to the pan and cook for a further 3 minutes, tossing the oysters with the bacon. Meanwhile, slice the warm bread and spread generously with butter. Top the bread with the bacon and oysters and serve immediately.

Cornbread comes in many different shapes, sizes, colours and textures. We prefer making the slightly less healthy version, which is fried rather than baked. It is absolutely delicious served with cured bacon and maple syrup, or with a barbecued rack of ribs. We've provided a few different flavouring ingredients to add to the basic mixture if you fancy a change.

MAKES 3

250g (8oz) cornmeal

3 teaspoons baking powder

1½ teaspoons salt

100g (3½oz) lard or bacon fat

120ml (just under 4fl oz) milk

120ml (just under 4fl oz) yoghurt

2 eggs, beaten

JALAPEÑO CORNBREAD

2 jalapeño chillies, finely diced

FRESH CORNBREAD

50g (2oz) sweetcorn kernels

CHICKPEA, LIME AND CORIANDER CORNBREAD

50g (2oz) canned chickpeas, rinsed and drained

zest and juice of 1 lime

1 tablespoon chopped fresh coriander

CORNBREAD

Preheat the oven to 200°C (400°F), Gas Mark 6. Place the cornmeal, baking powder, salt and any of your chosen flavouring ingredients in a large mixing bowl. Melt half the lard or bacon fat in a pan over a medium heat, then add the milk and yoghurt and heat until tepid. Pour into the mixing bowl with the beaten eggs and the dry ingredients and stir with a wooden spoon until fully incorporated.

Meanwhile, melt the remaining lard or bacon fat in an ovenproof skillet or heavy-based frying pan until starting to smoke. Place 3 metal rings, about 10cm (4 inches) in diameter, in the pan and pour the batter into the rings. Cook for 1–2 minutes, then transfer to the oven and cook for 20 minutes until golden brown. Slice and serve warm or cold.

Cheese scones have stood the test of time. No longer a risky option that encroaches on the territory of the sweet teatime scone, these savoury versions occupy their own space in the baking world. They sit perfectly on a summer picnic rug next to slices of cold meat and pickled onions. Our version uses crumbly cheese and walnuts, delicious with a spoonful of spiced apple chutney.

MAKES 8

500g (1lb) strong white flour, plus extra for dusting

75g (3oz) butter, softened, plus extra for greasing

240ml (7½fl oz) milk

30g (1¼oz) caster sugar

1 teaspoon salt

30g (1¼oz) baking powder

2 eggs, beaten, plus extra for brushing

100g (3½oz) Wensleydale or other crumbly cheese

50g (2oz) walnuts, whole or lightly broken into pieces

25g (1oz) Cheddar or Parmesan cheese, grated (optional)

CRUMBLY CHEESE SCONES

Place the flour and butter in a large mixing bowl, then rub the butter into the flour with the fingertips until the mixture resembles fine breadcrumbs. Stir in the milk, sugar, salt, baking powder and beaten eggs, then use your hands to form a rough dough. Turn the dough out on to a floured work surface and knead for 5–10 minutes or until smooth. Sprinkle the crumbly cheese and walnuts over the dough and work again for another few minutes until evenly distributed.

Shape the dough into a round about 25cm (10 inches) across. Transfer to a greased baking sheet and mark the loaf into 8 triangles with a knife, taking care not to cut all the way through the dough. Brush the top of the dough with beaten egg and leave to rest in the refrigerator for 30–40 minutes.

Preheat the oven to 200°C (400°F), Gas Mark 6. Brush with a little more egg and sprinkle with grated cheese, if using. Cook in the oven for about 25 minutes until golden. Allow to cool on a wire rack.

Any leftover scones can be wrapped in greaseproof paper and stored in a bread bin where they will stay fresh for 3–4 days. Refresh before eating by cooking in a preheated oven at 180°C (350°F), Gas Mark 4, for 4–5 minutes.

This farmhouse classic is an incredibly useful way to use up over-ripe bananas. Banana bread is best enjoyed on the day that it is baked -- it should have a soft inside and a crunchy, sugared crust. If you want more texture in your banana bread, use half wholemeal flour and half plain.

SERVES 6-8

FOR THE BANANA BREAD

175g (6oz) walnut pieces

4 ripe bananas

125g (4oz) butter, softened, plus extra for greasing

175g (6oz) soft brown sugar

2 eggs, beaten

225g (7½oz) plain flour

1 teaspoon ground cinnamon

a pinch of salt

1 heaped teaspoon baking powder

zest of 1 lemon

zest of 1 orange

1 tablespoon demerara sugar

FOR THE RUM BUTTER

1 tablespoon caster sugar

1 shot of white rum

100g (3½oz) butter, softened

BANANA BREAD

Preheat the oven to 180°C (350°F), Gas Mark 4, and grease a 1kg (2lb) loaf tin, or line it with a paper liner. Place the walnut pieces on a baking sheet and roast in the oven for about 10 minutes, taking care not to let them brown too much. Allow to cool a little, then roughly chop them.

Mash 3 of the bananas and chop the other into 1cm (½ inch) cubes. Cream the softened butter and soft brown sugar in a bowl until pale and fluffy, then add the eggs. Beat until smooth and then sift the flour, cinnamon, salt and baking powder into the bowl. Continue to beat until smooth, and then add the citrus zest. Fold in the roasted walnuts and bananas, then check the consistency. The mixture should drip off the spoon – if it is too thick, add a splash of milk.

Spoon the mixture into the prepared tin and sprinkle the demerara sugar over the top. Cook in the oven for 1¼–1½ hours, until a skewer inserted into the banana bread comes out clean. Leave to cool in the tin for 5 minutes before transferring to a wire rack.

Make the rum butter by simply creaming the sugar and rum with the softened butter until smooth. Thickly slice the bread while still warm and serve with the butter.

A spoonful of sugar makes all the difference

There are muffins that you buy and there are those that you make at home. Ours make the perfect family baking treat, especially if you head out and brave the brambles to forage for your own blackberries. Hazelnuts are also readily available in many hedgerows, but if you can't find them or it's the wrong time of year, just buy some.

MAKES 16

250g (8oz) butter, softened

175g (6oz) caster sugar

4 eggs, beaten

250g (8oz) strong white flour

2 teaspoons baking powder

75g (3oz) hazelnuts, crushed

250g (8oz) blackberries

1 teaspoon icing sugar

1 teaspoon ground cinnamon

HEDGEROW MUFFINS

Preheat the oven to 200°C (400°F), Gas Mark 6, and line a 16-hole muffin tin with paper cases. Cream the butter and sugar together in a mixing bowl using a wooden spoon, then add the beaten eggs and mix until smooth. Sift the flour and baking powder into the bowl and fold in until well combined. When the mixture is smooth, add the crushed nuts and stir lightly.

Divide the muffin mixture between the paper cases and arrange the blackberries on top, then press them down into the muffins so they are just beneath the surface. Cook in the oven for about 12 minutes, until risen and firm to the touch.

Cool on a wire rack, then dust the muffins with the icing sugar and cinnamon.

INDEX

15·10·13

ACKNOWLEDGEMENTS

AUTHOR ACKNOWLEDGEMENTS

I'd like to thank the following people: my beautiful wife Holly for recipe testing with me and holding the fort while I was writing; Indy for eating my bread and making it worth the hard work; my dad for supporting me; my mum for encouraging me and making the best toast in the world; my sister Charlotte for the amazing artwork and not being afraid to tell me less is more; my granny in Ireland for all Irish recipes; my granny and grandpa in Dorset for instilling a love of homemade bread; my mother-in-law for being nice about my cooking; Brett Camborne-Paynter, our favourite local chef, for helping us to bake at such short notice; all the photography team – Clare, Nick and Alison – for understanding our Made at Home family; Home Economics teacher Kim Tutcher for inspiring me; and Duncan Glendinning from the Thoughtful Bread Company for being my baking hero.

— *James Strawbridge*

PICTURE CREDITS

All photographs © **Nick Pope** with the exception of the following: **Monica Butnaru/Fotolia** (used throughout). **Strawbridge Family Archive** 13 ar, 155 ar. **iStockphoto/Thinkstock** (used throughout).

Illustrations: **Charlotte Strawbridge** 14, 42, 58, 84, 152. **James Strawbridge** 39.

Publisher: Stephanie Jackson
Managing Editor: Clare Churly
Copy-editor: Jo Smith
Creative Director: Jonathan Christie
Designer: Jaz Bahra
Illustrators: Charlotte Strawbridge, James Strawbridge
Photographer: Nick Pope
Stylist: Alison Clarkson
Assistant Production Manager: Lucy Carter

MADE AT HOME
DICK & JAMES STRAWBRIDGE

CURING & SMOKING

MADE AT HOME
DICK & JAMES STRAWBRIDGE

EGGS & POULTRY

MADE AT HOME
DICK & JAMES STRAWBRIDGE

VEGETABLES

MADE AT HOME
DICK & JAMES STRAWBRIDGE

PRESERVES